HARASSING THE DEVIL

Touching Hearts Changing Lives
through Short Term Missions

ROY CERNY

WESTBOW
PRESS®
A DIVISION OF THOMAS NELSON
& ZONDERVAN

WestBow Press books may be ordered through booksellers or by contacting:

WestBow Press
A Division of Thomas Nelson & Zondervan
1663 Liberty Drive
Bloomington, IN 47403
www.westbowpress.com
844-714-3454

Scripture taken from the King James Version of the Bible.

ISBN: 978-1-6642-5136-6 (sc)
ISBN: 978-1-6642-5137-3 (hc)
ISBN: 978-1-6642-5135-9 (e)

Library of Congress Control Number: 2021924077

Print information available on the last page.

WestBow Press rev. date: 01/05/2022

CONTENTS

PROLOGUE

There was a time not too many years ago when I gave short-term mission work no thought. I guess I didn't see the need, or I thought someone else would be better at doing it than I. Maybe no opportunities presented themselves, or perhaps the Lord was waiting for me to be willing, or maybe I just was too into myself and hadn't grown in my walk enough for Him to use me.

Today, people ask me why I go on mission trips and spend so much money for the travel expenses when I could just send the money to the needy or why I travel to distant places when there are so many in need here at home. I won't try to answer those questions but will leave it up to you, the reader, to find out for yourself as you read these short stories about my mission trips overseas and to areas in the United States.

ABOUT THE AUTHOR

Roy Cerny is a quiet, service-oriented guy who loves to help people. He finds joy in working to meet the needs of others. He is a veteran of short-term mission trips to Jamaica, Paraguay, Nepal, Mexico, and five different areas of Chile.

These trips involved church and home construction, evangelism, street ministry, teaching, and assisting missionaries and church leaders in each of the countries. In the United States, he and his friends traveled to storm-ravaged New Jersey to help rebuild homes. He also participated in numerous projects at his district Bible camp as well as helped with projects at his local church.

Now in his seventies, Roy feels the need to share his experiences in a book with the hope that others might experience the changes he has seen in his own life. These stories of his trips and projects, told chronologically, portray the growth of his faith as he opened himself up to be a useful instrument for the Lord. What he has seen and done, as told through his short stories, will hopefully build in the reader a desire to experience the life changes a mission trip can provide. The author is so emotionally tied to many of the experiences he depicts that he finds it difficult to relate the stories without tearing up from the memories. It is his hope that you will also find joy and satisfaction in letting the Lord take you where He needs you to be.

ABOUT THE TITLE

"Harassing the Devil" is a catchy title for a book, but standing alone, it would not lead a potential reader to believe it is a book about short-term missions. Thus, the subtitle, "Touching Hearts and Changing Lives through Short-Term Missions" needed to be added. I am not sure who coined the phrase "harassing the devil," but I know it was used as a sign-off on some of the emails that were sent back to the states when we were out of the country. My wife liked the phrase and encouraged me to use it as the book title. I hope it encourages you to read the book.

ABOUT THE COVER PHOTO

The unique lighted cross was constructed by the author for his home church, Eagan Hills Alliance. It is constructed out of chunks of wood blocks, branches, and assorted species of wood assembled on a wooden base. The unusual design of the cross is explained by the author as: The blocks of wood represent people, people who are of many races, backgrounds, ages, and at various stages of Christian growth. Many have had a rough time in life as evidenced by the broken blocks and the knots that have twisted their growth. Each one is unique, but all have found salvation by clinging to the cross of Christ, and together, they make up a fellowship of believers. Crosses come in many styles and forms, but they all represent God's greatest gift to mankind, His son, Jesus, who died in our place for the remission of our sins. All we have to do is believe in Him and accept His gift.

The cross quilt on the back cover was made by my wife, Midge and given to my friend Mark McCoy. He went on two mission trips to Chile and then on to his heavenly home.

ABOUT THE BOOK

This book is a combination of many experiences. It is an autobiography of a portion of nearly twenty-five years of the author's life. The stories are also a travelogue of places visited and new friends made, but most importantly, it is a book written to encourage others to be open to the leading of the Lord.

The book follows the author's growth as a Christian, from an almost reluctant participant in mission work to an eager worker for the Lord. It relates many eye-opening experiences of places and people, projects and missions both in and out of country.

The book is soul-touching, heart-warming, miracle-sharing, and hopefully, encouraging. At times funny, at other times serious, but always with eye-opening wonder, the book shares the many years of experiences of the author doing work for the Lord. It shows the growth of his faith, the strengthening of his beliefs, and the encouragement he has felt by letting the Lord use him in whatever way He can.

DEDICATION

I wish to thank family, friends, and team members who have put time and effort into arranging the details for the short-term mission trips in which I have been privileged to participate. In particular, I admire Sheryl Jacobson, a former high school student of mine, who dedicated many years of her life to serving the Lord in Chile. I also have gratitude for her husband, Kimm, who was the team leader on many of our trips. Pastor Dave Stapf deserves mention for getting teams put together for our first two trips. Pastor Carter McFarland, Pastor John Lingenfelder and Pastor Doug Clevenger from the Clarkfield Alliance Church as well as Pastor Bruce Konold from my home church in Eagan, Minnesota, deserve mention for their heart for missions. I salute the dedicated Alliance missionaries in the field who helped make our trips successful. I also give praise to the STEM (Short Term Evangelical Missions) organization for the work they do getting volunteers into the mission field. Samaritan's Purse is another great organization bringing help to the needy in Jesus name after hurricane Harvey in Texas. The Methodist Churches in New Jersey were very helpful in organizing volunteers after hurricane Sandy struck the east coast.

My book is a compilation of a lifetime of mission experiences. I am greatly indebted to my first wife, Kathryn (deceased); my wife, Midge; my grandson Zack and my daughter-in-law Cassi for their encouragement and for the hours they worked on the book. Their editing and computer skills were of great help in completing the book. My friend Parker West was an enormous help in picking fonts, sizing pictures, and organizing all the material I had loosely assembled into a completed work. I have to say the project would not have gotten finished without his skills and encouragement.

Hopewell, Jamaica

1992

Pastor Dave Stapf gave a presentation to the members of Calvary Memorial Alliance Church that a short-term mission trip opportunity was in the works. He had talked to the head of STEM (Short Term Evangelical Missions) and had expressed interest to them that a number of our members might like to participate in a two-week mission trip to Jamaica. At the time, STEM was sending out teams to Jamaica, Haiti, and Trinidad. STEM was a fairly new multidenominational organization that orchestrated all of the logistics of the trips and matched the skill sets of the teams with the needs in those three countries.

After Dave presented the idea to the church, he asked, "How many people are interested in going on the June trip?"

After a few seconds of subdued conversation, about fifteen hands were raised. My brother, Paul, and my wife, Kathy, raised their hands. She gave me a poke in the ribs, so I raised my hand too. Dave presented the planned time frame, projected costs, and the activities that we would be participating in. I felt the construction projects suited me best, but I was apprehensive about sharing my faith on the days that we would be doing street ministry. Dave scheduled the next meeting, and those interested were given guidance on how to write letters to raise support funds for the trip. I felt Kathy and I could pay our own way, so we wrote no letters. Years later, I discovered that it was pride that prevented me from giving others a chance to support us.

In subsequent meetings, we found out that we would be housed at a church school, and that not only would we be responsible for our own meals but also that all meals would have to be instant and easily made with the only available amenity, boiling water. With my canoe trips and Boy Scout camping experiences, I volunteered my expertise and became the semiofficial group cook. Richard, one of our team members, belonged to the army reserves and was able to requisition hundreds of MREs (meals ready to eat) for lunches and some suppers. We planned to go out and eat a number of suppers in town, but the MREs would help keep food costs low.

As the June departure date neared, Kathy and I were both getting pretty excited about the trip. Kathy dug out our duffel bags and started setting aside all the things that she thought we would need. We even got out the bathroom scale to weigh our luggage to make sure it wasn't going over the seventy-pound limit for each of the four duffel bags we were allowed to take. I had to keep reminding her that we also had to carry our share of the food. We packed tools for some of the carpentry projects as well as candy and gifts for the children.

Other than some canoe trips that had allowed us to briefly enter into Canada, this was the first trip to a foreign country that either of us had ever taken. Kathy got a passport because she thought it would help eliminate confusion. She had had last name changes due to adoption and a previous marriage. Travelers could enter Jamaica with only a birth certificate and a driver's license at the time, but she didn't want to take any chances. We packed medicines and other essentials as we would not have easy access to those basic needs.

Finally, the big day came for departure. The church gave us prayer support and a great sendoff. For a number of us in the group, it was our first ride on a jet. Without delay, we were at thirty thousand feet and winging our way south. We had a stopover and plane change in Miami and had to wait on the runway for nearly two hours. The rest of the flight was a bit bumpy, but finally, we landed at the Montego Bay Airport. The landing was smooth, but after departing from the Minneapolis-St. Paul International Airport, the airport in Jamaica, with only four gates, seemed small.

As soon as we stepped off the plane, the smell of airplane fuel hit us. Walking into the hot, humid air was like walking into a wall. June in Jamaica and June in Minnesota were not the same. Steve Schmidt and his wife, Cindy, our STEM leaders, met us at the airport. Our transportation was Steve's beat-up fifteen-passenger van and a much nicer large van belonging to his good friend. We loaded up our luggage and team members and headed inland a few miles to the small town of Hopewell, where the church and school were located.

Upon our arrival, we were shown to our quarters. The guys bunked in a downstairs back room of the school, and the gals had their own separate quarters. Ed and his wife Leanne, who were volunteers from our church, and Kathy and I climbed some pretty scary-looking concrete steps to our second-floor room. Only one thin pillar of concrete supported the three inch thick steps. To our amazement and relief, they held up. We assumed they must have had a lot of rebar in them. Once upstairs, we blew up our air mattresses and camped out on picnic tables in a big unfinished room above the school's main classroom. We discovered that in Jamaica none of the windows have screens, and at night, the mosquitoes feast on all exposed flesh. It was too hot to be in the sleeping bags, but there were too many bugs to be out of them. We were surprised to see it get dark at around six-thirty at night as opposed to nearly ten o'clock at night back home, but we realized we were a lot closer to the equator than we had been in Minnesota, so the length of days and nights are almost equal year-round. We planned for a devotion time after breakfast in the mornings, and afterward, we would find out what projects would be in store for that day. We slept fitfully that first night even though we were exhausted. The bugs, heat, humidity, and the all-night barrage of noise from barking dogs and crowing roosters kept us from getting a good night's sleep.

Upon arriving in the kitchen in the morning, I found it interesting that there were several geckos perched on the rough plaster walls. The kitchen stove was made of welded reinforcing rod with a rubber hose leading to a burner from a 100-pound propane cylinder in the corner. Pretty primitive!

We made a big pot of coffee and boiled water for oatmeal. With a hot cup of java in my hand, I looked for a big spoon to stir the oatmeal. When I opened the silverware drawer, I was horrified to spot a couple of three-inch cockroaches scurrying over the utensils as they tried to hide. I dumped the drawer on the floor and tried to stomp on the escaping vermin. When I finally got my foot on one, I slipped and spilled my coffee all over myself. There was so much bug under my shoe that I felt like I had stepped on a banana. Paul and I resolved that one of our projects would be to build bug-proof cupboards for the school kitchen.

After an inspirational devotion time, we sang some choruses and then began to organize for the day. Steve and Cindy planned for some of our team to go out to do street ministry.

Those with construction experience, including Paul and me, got to go to the pastor's house to build a set of stairs to his upstairs apartment. Ed and several of the other guys worked on trying to repair the starter on the rickety old STEM fifteen-passenger van.

While Paul and I were assessing our project and noticing the buildings around us, we were amazed by the extensive concrete construction, with reinforcing rod hanging out the sides and roofs. The reinforcing rod left sticking out everywhere was to connect future additions onto the buildings. Steve said concrete is used extensively due to the termites that destroy wood structures, and that the island country is also highly susceptible to hurricane damage. Even though most of the construction was masonry, Hurricane Gilbert had inflicted considerable damage to many houses several years before. Paul and I spent the day buying termite-proof lumber and building stair supports and steps to the pastor's humble house, for which he was so grateful.

After our first morning of work, we gathered for lunch in the kitchen of the school to try MREs for the first time. Most thought they weren't too bad. They even came with towelettes to wipe our hands and little drink-mix packets. Each MRE had a different entrée, so we traded with each other to get our favorite parts.

At supper time, we gathered to eat and share our day's experiences. We all spoke about how the Jamaicans could quite easily understand us, as they also spoke English, but they had their own way of phrasing that often was not easily understood by us. We also shared how thankful we were that STEM had engaged the services of six young men to go out with the groups to help us understand the language as we encountered people and to serve as guides to keep us from getting lost. Each of us at supper stated how amazed we were by the lush greenery, the brightly colored flowers, and the unusual trees and shrubs we saw growing everywhere. We had each learned a bit about the Rastafarians, their voodoo religion, and marijuana smoking. We talked about the banana plantations we saw and the ore ships that hauled bauxite aluminum ore away for processing. Bauxite, bananas, and Blue Mountain Coffee were important exports for the Jamaican economy. Tourism was also a crucial source of island income, so we weren't surprised to see several giant cruise ships in the harbor.

Jim Krech and I shared that we had been startled by a man who rose up out of the ocean a few feet from us as we sat in prayer that morning down by the ocean. He had on snorkeling gear and had a fish he had speared for his breakfast. We all talked about how we were getting to see the real Jamaica and meet the everyday people. Most tourists seemed never to venture far enough away from the beaches to get to know the people.

The next day, Paul and I worked on the cupboards and were surprised that the only lumber available was all green treated. Anything else just didn't last. Despite the issues with the wood, we made the kitchen a bit more usable and safer with what we built.

That night, we participated in a church service with the local congregation. They all came dressed in their best clothes. We got to eat out at the Pork Pit, a local inexpensive eatery, and discovered a Chinese bakery nearby that had fresh bread in loaves that must have weighed three pounds each. We found that there were no preservatives in the bread and it became moldy after only two days in the heat and humidity. While in town, we looked for Mountain Dew (my drink of choice) but found that there was none available in Jamaica, so we had to settle for a carbonated pineapple flavored soda called Zing. It was pretty good. Because of our souvenirs we bought as we wandered around in town we were beginning to understand the monetary conversion of twenty-two Jamaican dollars equaling one American dollar.

On the third day of our stay at the school, the water pump for the whole city of Hopewell broke down. There was no running water in the city for the next seven days of the trip. If this had happened at home, there would have been a huge up-roar. The Jamaicans took it in stride and waited in line with their bottles and jugs for water from trucks. We traveled up into the hills and got water from a spring for cooking. The toilets were another matter.

We made several trips a day down to the ocean, which was two blocks away, with pairs of five-gallon pails so we could get water to flush the toilets. It was a lot of work. After several days without showers, we were getting a little ripe. A sudden thunderstorm one afternoon provided roof runoff water, which sent us scampering for our swimming suits so we could stand under the gutters and get a shower. Showers were not possible during that the rest of that week, as we could use only a dishpan of water Steve rationed daily to each of us from the cistern to wash up and brush our teeth.

The next day, we all went to visit the Little Blossom Children's Home. There were thirty-eight kids at the home who had been orphaned or whose parents couldn't care for them. With only two nurses to care for them, they were starved for affection and human touch. We spent hours just holding them. We passed out candy and gifts, and we were all touched to tears by how much they appreciated our time.

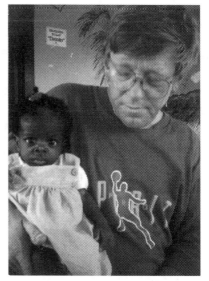

Talking about our visit afterward was difficult because we all had lumps in our throats as we related how we felt about the plight of the children. After sharing our stories and reflecting on the impact of our experiences, we decided to go shopping for souvenirs to take home. The market place was a series of tiny shops that specialized in certain items like hats and tee shirts. Prices were inexpensive but we knew any money we spent would help bolster the economy and we needed some cheering up.

Our next project was a visit to a new church called the Faith Deliverance Centre. The church was in an old building that used to be a maintenance shed for a Canadian road construction company. Our team built benches for their Sunday school program. Someone suggested to them that we could paint a large sign for the front of the building so those passing by would know that it was a church. They agreed to the idea, so off we went to find paint and plywood.

We discovered that even though the USA is close, there weren't that many American goods traded to Jamaica. The paint we found, which was all high gloss oil with a limited color selection, came from Trinidad.

We worked on the sign for the rest of that day and into the next. When we were done painting the sign, the church attendees were surprised to see us put all three panels up, making their new sign twenty-four feet long by four feet high. Passersby could definitely tell it was a church then.

We went to an old folks' home the next day. Forewarned by Steve, we had brought disposable razors to give shaves and scissors to give haircuts to the men who were housed in a separate building from the women. The gals in our group went to the women's section. We shaved heads and trimmed toenails and visited with the men. Pastor Dave just couldn't clip toe nails, so I teamed up with him and told him I would do it so that he could just visit with the men.

There was an empty coffin in the lobby of the men's building, which made us suspect it was the only way any of these men got to leave this facility. When we went in, one of the men was getting a shower from a garden hose held by a nurse in an open room with no door. Not much privacy and very little dignity was shown to these poor cast-offs from society. Most of them got few visitors and were eager to talk to us about what we were doing. We were moved by how content most of them were even though all they had to their name was the cot they slept on and perhaps a cardboard shoebox with their meager belongings inside under their bed. We spent about three or four hours with the men.

When we got back together with the gals, they shared the similar experiences they had had with the elderly women in the other building. We all cried as we realized how much we had and how blessed we were, especially compared to how little they had and yet were content and loved the Lord.

Steve and Cindy took us to a beautiful beach that afternoon to cheer us up. The white sand and palms were unlike anything we had in Minnesota. The sun was brutal, so we lathered up in sunscreen. Kathy and I rented snorkeling gear and swam in the crystal-clear water, seeing many varieties of fish. We ended with a nice dinner at a restaurant in Montego Bay, capping off an extremely memorable day.

All of our building projects had been completed, and it was my time to go out and witness to people on the street. Ed White and I teamed up with one of the interpreters and headed out to talk to people about Jesus. We carried Bibles and walked the streets. I was filled with dread, as I had never done this before. At the interpreter's urging, we began to talk to people who we met.

We shared the good news of the gospel and asked the question, "Would you like to accept Jesus right here and now?" To our amazement, only one person of the twenty or so we talked to said they were too busy to listen to us. All the others took the time to sit down with us and hear what we had to say. Seven people prayed the prayer to accept Christ. We were overjoyed at the working of the Spirit.

As our time in Jamaica was winding down, we took one day to travel around the island to try to further understand what Jamaican life was like. We chartered a bus and drove up the coast to a place called Fern Gully. It was a road that led up into the foothills through a gully, which was lined with overhanging trees, vines, and moss. It was like a rain forest. Many of the locals had small stands made of bamboo and tarps where they sold trinkets and handicrafts. As our bus pulled over at a scenic vista, a Jamaican man riding along side of the bus on an overloaded bicycle quickly dismounted by our bus door. His bike had a big cooler full of beer and featured a mat framework over the handlebars, which opened up like a miniature store-front.

I was the first one off the bus, and he waved me over, holding up a cold can of beer for sale. I shook my head no and said to him that we were a church group. Disappointment instantly replaced his look of enthusiasm, and he hastily folded up his portable store and pedaled away to find business elsewhere.

We continued traveling along the coast of the ninety-mile-long island to Ocho Rios, where there is a beautiful waterfall and rapids. We all changed into our swim suits and spent a delightful couple of hours wading up the rapids and standing under the falls. A young gal, Tara, in our group wanted to be baptized by Pastor Dave in the falls, so we took the time to do so joyously. She will remember that for the rest of her life.

As we walked back to the bus, I noticed some big black spots in the air below the branches of a banyan tree in the parking area. I checked my glasses and saw that they weren't dirty. As I got closer, I realized they were gigantic spiders with bodies about the size of hen eggs. Kathy gave the tree a pretty wide berth. We drove on down the coast passing several mansions belonging to famous singers and fashion designers.

That night we packed up our gear and spent the night at a local hotel with air conditioning!! How we had missed that! We met in the banquet room for a final meal together. It was a feast, but I couldn't enjoy it. I had come down with a bug and had to go back to our room. That night I had a fever that broke, and I saturated the sheets with sweat. I felt weak but better the next day.

We made the trip to the airport and spent time saying tearful goodbyes to our new friends. On the plane trip home, exhaustion overtook most of us, and we slept soundly until landing in Minneapolis. Many people from our church were there to greet us as we disembarked. We had been touched by the Lord during our time in Jamaica in ways that each of us would carry in our hearts for the rest of our lives. We all felt that as much as we had tried to do for the Lord, the Lord blessed us far more.

When we got home, I tried to get back to working on my landscaping project in the back yard. I struggled with the thought of how much the timbers had cost and how much good could have been done for the poor in Jamaica if those dollars had been spent helping them. I had a new appreciation for all the blessings the Lord had bestowed on us as Americans.

Asunción, Paraguay

1994

Pastor Dave Stapf had said to the STEM (Short Term Evangelical Missions) organization that our church would be interested in another mission trip after the great time we had in Jamaica in 1992. Soon, we heard that they were setting us up for another trip, this time to Paraguay. This was the first group that STEM was sponsoring to that country, so we would be breaking new ground.

At the first meeting of those interested in going, we found out that we would be doing construction work at a seminary being built forty miles outside of Asunción, the capitol city. We would be working under Richard Gwinn, an independent missionary with a vision to teach local men to be pastors. Richard also aimed for the seminary to teach them a skill such as carpentry or cooking, for example, that they could use to support themselves until they could grow their churches into self-supporting congregations.

The trip to Jamaica two years earlier had cost less than nine hundred dollars per person, and Kathy and I had paid our own way. During the meeting about the Paraguay trip, I learned that this mission trip would cost twice as much.

I leaned over to Kathy and whispered in her ear, "There is no way that we are going. We can't come up with that much cash." She looked at me with a smile and said, "We're going."

After twenty five years of marriage I had learned that once she had her mind made up, arguing would be useless, but I also knew we couldn't afford the trip. I wanted to go but knew it wasn't in my power. I was not yet ready to put it in God's hands. Kathy and I argued over the next month or so about how we might be able to afford it. Being stubborn and too proud to write letters to congregation members for support, I wrote the trip off. We just couldn't do it. Kathy continued to talk to our friends about our upcoming trip and began to gather things to take along and ignored my arguments against going. She knew we could not afford it but had a strong enough faith to know that somehow God would make it possible. I just fumed about where the money was going to come from.

She confidently said, "The Lord will provide funds if your heart is right and you have faith." She had already tucked away a considerable sum and a few friends had contributed to the cause. I just said, "Right. We'll see."

A week or so later, I got a letter from my parents. It was newsy, and they talked about what they were up to. Inside the letter was a check for five thousand dollars that they said was a gift. They had sent a check to each of my sisters and my brother as well. They stated in the letter for us to use it wisely–pay our bills or maybe start a retirement plan. They had no idea we were thinking of going to Paraguay. It was an answer to Kathy's fervent prayer to go on this mission trip. I think she knew her days were numbered because she had been battling breast cancer for several years. The generosity of my parents paid our current bills with enough left over to finish paying our costs to go on the mission trip. Kathy's dream, and now mine as well, of going on the mission trip became a reality in spite of my doubtfulness. It was settled; we were going!

Later, on a Sunday morning, Dave called all those going on the trip up to the front of the church. He asked each of us get up and say a few words about how the fundraising was going. The team was made up of three married couples, Pastor Dave and his son, several other church members, and a couple young folks. When I got up and told the story of how the Lord had almost magically supplied our support for the trip from many sources, I was so broken by my sin of pride and stubbornness that I completely broke down in tears and Kathy had to help finish what I was going to say.

⋊ 11 ⋉

The devil assailed us as plans were made. Kathy's cancer had come back. She had undergone five regimens of chemotherapy and more radiation. It had slowed the cancer, but I believe she knew it was terminal and that it would be only a matter of time. She really wanted to do this one last mission trip.

Five weeks before departure, she was at work at her veterinary tech job and took a large dog outside on a leash to walk him. The dog spotted a squirrel and bolted, jerking her around. She heard her leg snap as she went down. Another tech spotted her and carried her back inside. They x-rayed her leg, saw the broken bone, and called me. I rushed over and took her to the hospital. The doctors told her the cast would have to be on for six to eight weeks. She argued saying, "No way! I'm going to Paraguay in five weeks. You have to figure out a way the cast can come off sooner." The doctor said that if the break was pinned, she could have the cast off just before departure, as healing would be sped up. "Go for it," she said. She was stubborn and cut the cast off herself after suffering with it for only four weeks. A few weeks before we were to leave, the airline we were booked on went bankrupt, so new last minute travel plans had to be made. Our flight was now going to St Louis, then Miami, and finally to Santiago, Chile, with a long layover before going back up to the northeast to Asunción, Paraguay. The devil had been hard at work trying to disrupt what we were trying to do for the Lord. We asked everyone to continue to pray for the team and for all the plans to be put in the Lord's hands.

The departure date finally came. We had a church prayer time and a great sendoff. Our team had fourteen members. Our leaders were Dave

and Nancy Carlson from another church. Counting them, Ed and Leanne White, and Kathy and me, we had three married couples. Jim Krech took his son, Jesse, and our Pastor Dave Stapf took his son Dale. Richard Cady, who had supplied all the MREs for the Jamaica trip, came along. Two young girls, Michelle Krech, Jims niece, and Kathy Aune, from our church, and Boyd Kodama, who joined us after flying in from Philadelphia, rounded out the team.

We made it to St. Louis fine, but after our plane change, we were held up by the threat of severe weather and took off after an hour's delay. The delay was going to make it tough to make our connecting flight in Miami.

When we got there, we found they had held the flight for us, and we were rushed to the plane and boarded just in time. The flight to Santiago was nine hours long, and then we had a nine-hour layover before our flight to Asunción. That flight was also delayed a few hours while they worked to repair the aircraft. As we walked down the tarmac to board, we saw that the nose cone of the jet had been taken off, and a man was standing on a tall stepladder banging loudly on something with a hammer. We boarded, and they finished putting the plane back together. Right after takeoff, the plane banked into a sharp turn and headed northeast right at the snow-covered Andes Mountains. Finally, it gained enough altitude to clear them. I was a bit white knuckled. After another six hours of flying, we landed in Asunción. Twenty-nine total hours of travel time! It was supposed to be winter in Paraguay, but it was over ninety degrees when we landed.

Richard and his wife, Elly, and a good friend of his, Steve Jones, met us at the airport. Steve had a large passenger van. Most of the team

was put up in Richard and Elly's house, and some went to his friend Stephen's home. We were able to take showers, eat a good meal, and get some badly needed rest.

The next day, Richard drove us forty miles out to his seminary that he called "The Ranch." He led us to our quarters, a small two-story house and an outbuilding with some bunks, which housed all the single folks. The outbuilding had a thatched roof about a foot thick. The house next to it had a small kitchen, which Richard had stocked with some food items and several bedrooms for the married couples.

Richard showed us around the forty acre property, and we talked about the project. He had planned for us to lay bricks. We were willing but had no experience doing that. When he found out that our teams skills included plumbing, electrical, and carpentry work, he was delighted. He quickly changed plans and went shopping for materials for us to work with and bought additional groceries for us to eat. The main building was already erected and needed plumbing and wiring done. Richard hired bricklayers from town for three dollars a day to lay the walls for the dormitories.

Several Christian ladies from town came out and cooked a supper of spaghetti noodles smothered in cheese sauce with about a half-pound chunk of lean beef on top for us. On the side, we had a vegetable, which the locals ate like potatoes, but we thought tasted more like parsnips. The hot weather turned chilly in the evening (to the point we had to put on jackets), and we ate outside on top of a ping-pong table.

Richard had diverted a small creek that ran out of the foothills into a rock pool he had built, which was about five feet deep and twenty feet long. He said we could bathe in it. A couple of brave souls tried the pool but found the water to be about fifty degrees. Deciding on a more  comfortable option for bathing, we hung up a black tarp, with men showering on one side and women on the other. We heated water in a fifty-gallon barrel over a wood fire and poured it into overhead pails that had lots of holes in the bottoms. We only got about a sixty-second hot shower per bucket, but it was a lot better than the pool.

 In the morning, we made hot oatmeal, toast, and coffee in the small kitchen and again ate out on the ping-pong table. We had fresh squeezed juice made from oranges the gals had picked off a tree in the yard. The small yard of the homestead was fenced in and had

an outside sink where we took turns doing the dishes. It also had a big brick barbeque as well as an oven built like a mud igloo.

Richard had never used the oven, so we asked him if he would buy us a couple of cake mixes so we could try it out. On the edge of the yard was a large poly barrel perched about twenty-five feet up on a platform supported by sturdy poles. It served as a gravity-fed water tower to supply running water for the buildings. It was filled with water pumped up from the spring that also fed water to the small creek.

We found out the yard was fenced to keep the cows out. The ranch sported a herd of cattle that lingered just outside the fence, eating

the oranges that fell on their side of the fence. The ranch had numerous citrus trees as well as many coconut palms. Later in the week, we saw men harvesting the golf ball sized coconuts that were exported for their oil. The oil was used as an ingredient in suntan lotion, shampoos, and soaps. Beef, leather, and exotic hardwoods were other things that Paraguay exported.

Out in the country and away from the capitol city, we felt we had been transported back to the American west of the 1880s. There were gravel roads, but riding horseback was the common means of transportation.

We saw lots of cowboys and even oxen pulling oxcarts loaded with goods. Richard had hired a local man to be the caretaker and watchman of the property. He came every morning, riding bareback on his horse.

The property had several thickets of large six-foot-high cacti and many termite mounds that stood about three feet tall. In the distance, past the open grassy pastures, were small hills covered with trees.

We went to work the next day, stringing plastic conduit for wiring and locating electrical boxes. The channels for the conduit were scratched into the soft adobe brick with claw hammers, and the flexible plastic conduit was anchored by tapping in two nails into the bricks at an angle forming an X. The boxes for the outlets were nailed into the adobe and then further anchored with a mix of dirt, Portland cement, and water. This mud mortar was mixed with hoes right on the ground. After the wiring was installed, the conduit and boxes would be  buried in stucco. We made the stucco by mixing five shovels of termite mound dirt with one shovel of Portland cement.

Wiring in Paraguay would not pass code in Minnesota. Each building had only one hot wire running to it. Under the direction of Dave Carlson, our team electrician, we wired the circuits and then neutral was run to earth ground with a copper rod. There was no protective ground wire. The voltage was 240 at fifty cycles. Apparently, this is standard for most of South America. The wires seemed awfully thin to be carrying that much current. It took two days, but we got the entire large meeting room wired for lights and outlets and fired them up with a Honda generator.

That night, a local evangelical group came out, played guitars, and sang. They gave an interesting presentation using fluorescent chalk that they lit up with an ultraviolet light. People from the area were invited, but the five-inch rainstorm we had that day made road travel difficult and few came.

The hot weather we had had at the beginning of the week was broken by the heavy rain, and now it felt like fall in Minnesota. We could see our breath in the morning, but daytime temps got into the sixties. We worked for the next five days on the big building. We broke up scrap brick and spread them out over the floor to make a base for the concrete that would be poured later. We assembled and buried the sewer lines that were made of lightweight PVC pipe. Elbows and bends were made by heating the pipe with an old-fashioned gasoline blowtorch until it was soft and then bending it to the desired shape. Soon all the plumbing

was in. It never got cold enough to worry about frost, so everything was buried quite shallow. In the kitchen area, we installed rafters and put in a ceiling out of tongue and groove boards. It looked pretty good after we varnished it.

Our team leader Dave saw that the power pole, which was a few hundred yards from the main building, had a number of dangerous, dangling wires at the main electric

shutoff. He thought the wires might electrocute the cows. On the pole were two large cartridge fuses with hooks on them that we would have to pull on to disconnect the power. Richard said the lines were 14,000 volts. Dave tried to pull the fuses to the off position with a dry

bamboo pole but felt a shock through the nails in his shoe soles. It wasn't dangerous, but he couldn't get the fuses off, so Richard called in some local electricians to disconnect them. They came barefoot on horseback with a little toolbox. Wearing no protective gear, they got the fuses off, and then we were able to clean up the loose wires and make the box safe. I don't think they have an OSHA in Paraguay.

On our time off, we enjoyed our short hot showers and got to bake two chocolate cakes in the igloo oven. It wasn't a Betty Crocker cake mix, but they were quite good. We even tried out the barbeque pit. We got to have a couple of campfires in the hills at night and enjoyed a big full moon. Each morning, Kathy would get up early and limp up the hill to watch the sunrise and pray. She would take her flute, and at the appropriate time, she would begin to play. It served as a most pleasant alarm clock that woke the rest of us up. A couple of the teenagers didn't wake up that easily and had to be persuaded a bit to rise. When we were all awake, we took turns leading a short Bible study to start the day off right. The time at the ranch went fast, and we  were growing to love the quiet times away from the hustle and bustle of the Twin Cities.

One afternoon, Richard said he would like to take us to a neighboring town to do some shopping and go for a ride on an old locomotive and have a picnic. We left in Stephen's big van and Richard's beat-up Land Rover. We had to disconnect the front drive shaft on the Rover because of a bad U-joint. The Rover also had broken springs, so it went down the road leaning at about a ten-degree angle. We couldn't get parts to fix it, so we solved the problem by putting the heavier people in our group on the uphill side of the vehicle to counterbalance it.

We stopped for a bite to eat at a roadside hamburger joint that had their menu posted on the front. I ordered a "hamburguestas especial" for forty-seven hundred gaunarines (their dollars). The equivalent cost in U.S. currency was about two dollars. Mighty cheap for what I got. While we waited for the food, a rooster strolled in through the open front door–clucking away–and out the back. When my order arrived, I had protein overload! Besides the large, lean hamburger patty, there was a slab of ham–a half-inch-thick; a layer of bacon; then between each layer was a fried egg; with a couple of slices of cheese to top off the whole sandwich.

Once we arrived at the train station, we had to chase a sleeping sow pig off the porch so we could get in to buy our tickets. While we waited for the train to arrive, we engaged a bunch of local kids in a spirited soccer match. It was great fun, even with the language barrier. A couple of people in our group could speak a bit of Spanish, so we thanked them for the game as we heard the whistle of our train coming. Seemingly right out of an old western movie, a wood-fired steam locomotive pulled up. We piled into the first passenger car. It had wooden bench seats. As we took off, sparks from the wood-fired boiler came flying in the windows. We were constantly patting them out, trying to keep them from burning holes in our clothes.

In the back corner of the car was a walled-off area without a door. Curious, I peeked in. Inside was an eight-inch hole in the floor with two red footprints painted in front of it. The footprints had no front or back, so I guess the hole was for whatever nature was calling one to do. We rode on the narrow-gauge train for about twenty miles to the stationhouse.

Our team was taken on a tour of the facility where the trains were repaired. Paraguay was trying to revive the old trains for tourism. The system had been set up by the British over one hundred years ago, and they had only a couple of the engines up and running. The yard around the building was littered with old engines and parts. Inside, three train boilers had been set up in tandem to provide steam power to spin a long drive shaft near the ceiling. It had large belts running down, which powered metal lathes, drills, and other pieces of machinery to make and repair parts for the trains. The tour was quite interesting even though we couldn't understand most of what was said in Spanish.

After the instructional tour, we were treated to a picnic lunch and then got a ride back to the depot with Stephan. It was an interesting afternoon. We spent time in town shopping for souvenirs and sampling different kinds of foods. Because refrigeration was such a luxury, most meat was heavily salted to help preserve it, and the favorite preparation method was to barbeque it. If we ate a lot of it, our tongues began to hurt from all the salt.

We had another campfire back at the ranch that night, and the clear starlit sky was spectacular. Living in the Twin Cities, we didn't get to see the stars like this. None of our familiar constellations were out of course because we were south of the equator, but we were able to find the Southern Cross. We also saw numerous meteors. Richard promised us a special touring expedition the next day, so we turned-in to be ready for an early start.

Very early the next morning, we boarded two small vans that Richard had arranged for our trip and then set out to drive for five hours to the border of Brazil and Venezuela. We encountered a traffic jam there. Our driver's name was Arnold. He was from Austria. He could have been Arnold Schwarzenegger's brother. He was the same size, had the same accent, and the same build. He kept us on pins and needles by how close he tailgated others and how fast he drove.

After the long ride, we came to the first of the places Richard wanted us to see. It was a great power dam built across the large river that forms the border between Brazil and Paraguay. It took ten years to build and cost 10 billion dollars. It was five miles long and seven hundred feet high. It formed a lake two hundred and fifty miles long. The three raceways for the excess water ran to the side of the powerhouse. At the base of the concrete sluices, the water was shot up into the air to keep erosion to a minimum. The nineteen penstock pipes that carried the water into the interior of the dam were each thirty-two feet in diameter. Each penstock fed its huge volume of water to a nine thousand ton turbine electrical generator. Just two generators provided enough power for almost all of Paraguay. Nine others supplied Brazil with about a quarter of their country's power needs. The rest of the power produced was sold to other South American countries. 500-thousand-volt powerlines distributed the power. The dam was built in a cooperative effort by the government of the two countries. Until the completion of the Aswan Dam in Egypt, it was the largest dam ever built. It was quite a sight.

We drove about another fifty miles to see Iguazu Falls. A large river, which spreads out over a flat mesa, formed this waterfall. In the middle of the mesa was a large gorge that is six hundred feet deep. The water poured over the edge in over two hundred separate cataracts on both sides of the gorge.

We walked on a trail on one side of the cliff, taking dozens of pictures, but the best was yet to come. Our walkway went around a last corner and terminated at a scenic lookout

perched on the edge of a three hundred-foot chasm. This main part of the falls is called "The Devil's Throat." On one side of the fifteen-foot observation platform, a three hundred-foot-high waterfall was pouring down on the ledge that the walkway was perched on so precariously.

Looking to the right, only thirty feet away, the water spilled over the edge and dropped another three hundred feet into a churning cauldron. The aluminum walkway and lookout area we stood on trembled with the power of the tumbling water and we had to shout to be heard. I wished I had rented a raincoat from the Paraguayan vendor we had passed on the trail, because my clothes and camera were soon soaked with the mist coming off the falls. These falls were over twice the height of Niagara and covered two miles in length. It was breathtaking.

The plants in the gorge were like those in a rainforest because of the unending supply of mist. The sun made numerous rainbows as we peered through the clouds of vapor thrown up by the tumbling water. We walked back to a fork in the walkway, which led to an

elevator that took us to the top of the falls. There we found numerous critters the locals called coatimundi. The critters looked like a cross

between our raccoons and an anteater. They were quite tame and begged for food. When Ed tried to give one a small bite of a candy bar, he was accosted by about a dozen of them who fought over the morsel. They started climbing up Ed, trying to get more. We backed up giving them some space. It had been an interesting and exciting day. We all agreed that we had never seen anything on earth as beautiful as the falls. It has to be one of the great wonders of the world. After an amazing day, we began our long drive home. It took longer going home in the dark. The lights on one of the vans began to dim due to some unknown electrical problems. We finally got to bed about one in the morning with dreams of the wondrous creation of God in our heads.

The next day, we traveled back to Asunción to go to work for a few days in a Salvation Army-sponsored orphan home. The home had thirty-eight children of various ages and was in dire need of repairs. We spent two days fixing doors, toilets, ceiling fans, and whatever else we could find that was broken. We painted the dining hall and the pantry. The gals put on a puppet show for the children. The dining hall had only a bag of oatmeal and a big bag of pancake mix in it. A stray dog was sleeping on the bottom shelf of the empty cupboard.

When the gals left to perform their puppet show at another orphanage, the guys on our team put their heads together. We decided to pool some of our extra spending money and make a trip to the farmer's market to see what we could get to supplement the meager supply of food we had seen for the children. We found out that the home was in pretty bad financial shape and could barely pay their bills.

The Uruguayan woman who was the director of the orphanage had at first not wanted us to come because she said they had no funds to buy the materials and paint to do the needed repairs. She gladly changed her mind when Richard told her that we were providing the money to buy the necessary items. With all the guys pitching in, we came up with 180 U.S. dollars that we exchanged for 336 thousand Paraguayan dollars. At the market, we went crazy with that much money. We bought crates of oranges and other fruits and vegetables. We found fresh tomatoes and bought a bushel. We bought eggs by the hundreds. We loaded big bags of flour, sugar, cocoa, and powdered milk. Finally, we had spent all the money. We loaded eight hundred pounds of food into the old Land Rover and began the trip back to the orphanage. As we made our way back, I thought about how that much food in the USA would have cost many times the amount we had paid.

The director and the children had already said their tearful thank yous and goodbyes to our group and wondered why we had returned. We shouldered the bags, boxes, and crates of food, then marched back into the orphanage, heading right for the pantry. The director burst into tears seeing what we had done, and we soon joined her, all of us crying joyful tears. The children were wiping away tears, too, but all had big smiles knowing they would not be hungry for quite a while. Richard Cady gave additional money, telling the director to buy more food when this was gone. He also got the address of the home so he could send more to them for food later. The children all lined up, and we had to walk the gauntlet again, giving hugs and kisses to all a second time as we said our final goodbye to them.

After all these years, I still tear up and get a lump in my throat as I tell the story of the children in the orphanage. The Lord has so blessed America, and we should be thankful to Him.

We ended the last of our days in Paraguay with a banquet at a big restaurant. It was much like an Old Country Buffet, except for the meat. All the fruits, vegetables, and salads were self-serve, but numerous waiters brought the meat to us on kabobs. There was chicken, beef, pork, fish, goat, several kinds of sausages, and I think several other kinds of mystery meats. It was all heavily salted but cooked to perfection. They just kept bringing more. We felt like gluttons, especially after knowing how little the less fortunate had to eat. The bill came to over three hundred thousand Paraguayan dollars, which came out to be only twelve U.S. dollars each.

We boarded our plane at the airport later that day. Our flight home had none of the delays we had experienced on our flight down. It still took twenty-two hours of travel time to get back to Minnesota. We were met at the airport by about thirty congregation members. It felt great to be home, but we all had a special place in our hearts for all the people we had met in Paraguay.

In a way, it was depressing to leave the simple life in that country and come home to the stress and pressure that we faced every day in our homes and jobs. A trip to a country such as Paraguay is like a trip back in time, where hugs, smiles, and handshakes mean something, and life is simpler and closer to the Creator. Our materialism stands out in stark contrast to their way of life. The things we value and what we spend our money on are never-to-be-known luxuries for most of the people in the world. It is good to contemplate what our dollars really could buy that would make such a difference in the world and for the Lord if we would just choose to share them with the less fortunate.

Temuco, Chile

2000

In April of 1996, my wife of twenty-six years, Kathy, went to her heavenly home after an eight-year battle with cancer. She had been able to make the mission trip to Paraguay in 1994, but I believe she knew her time on earth was winding down. She had endured a lot of suffering with all the chemotherapy regimens and had even gone through an autologous bone marrow transplant procedure to no avail. The cancer continued to grow in her lymph nodes and entered her lungs. In her last years, she taught me a lot about how to live for God and, in her last few weeks, how to die gracefully. Thankfully, she was bedridden for only the last two days of her life. With the help of the wonderful hospice workers, she was able to give a testimony at church and to spend time with her brother, sisters, and family before saying goodbye.

After her death, I felt a great emptiness and filled it by immersing myself in my work and activities. I grew much closer to my son, Matt, and went on numerous hunting and canoe fishing trips. I tried to be a good grandpa to my grandkids, Zachary and Rebeccah. I did all I could to fill the void, buying an old Jaguar to fix up and adding many guns to my firearm collection. I quit my apartment maintenance job and decided to start my own contracting business. With all the activity, there was still emptiness. I stayed active in church, and I must say without my church family, my grief would have overtaken me. Still, I had a longing to do more for the Lord.

In the late fall of 2000, I got a phone call from Steve Larson from Echo, Minnesota. Steve was a former high school student of mine when I taught school there back in the late seventies. It was great to hear from him. He explained that the purpose of his call was to ask if I would consider going on a short-term mission trip to southern Chile with him and a number of church members from the Alliance Church in Echo. I knew most of those going because many were former students. It made me really feel my age when I found out that two of them were taking their teenage children. Steve explained that their group had lost a couple of those going because of unforeseen circumstances and there was room for me. None of them had ever been on a mission trip before, and they knew I had, so they felt my experience with mission trips would be valuable to them.

The trip involved construction work, and he felt it would be perfect for me to go. He said Sheryl Ottoson, who was also a former student of mine, was a missionary for the Alliance Church in the area we were going to. I hadn't seen Sheryl in the nearly twenty years she had served on the mission field. It didn't take much to convince me that the Lord was speaking to me in a loud voice–saying, "Go for it." I told Steve I would think about it but called him back the next night saying I would like to go. I had no idea how I would raise the money on short notice, but from past experience, I knew the Lord would provide.

I attended a couple of meetings in Echo as the group made plans. Our team leader explained that the ticket money was due soon. We would fly to Miami and then directly to Santiago. At Santiago, we would have a few hours of layover time and then board a flight to the southern Chilean town of Temuco. We would stay there for one week, building a chapel for the Mapuchi Indians, who lived just a few miles outside of town. The second week, we would drive further south to the town of Lago Ranco and build a second small church for the Indians living there. It sounded exciting. I had a great time at the planning meetings, renewing friendships with my former students, who were now in their early forties.

As fundraising was now critical, I wrote letters to friends inviting them to participate in this venture with prayer and with their gifts if they felt led by the Lord. My local church took a special offering as well.

The money came in, and along with what I had set aside, I had more than enough. The Lord provided what was needed and then some.

Mission trips are costly, but many people take them during their paid vacation time. For someone who is self-employed like me, it is more complicated because there is no paid time off, only a break in the income flow. The trip expenses must also include the wages that are lost by taking the time off. Such was the case with me. A trip of two weeks that costs fifteen hundred dollars also incurs wage loss of up to an additional two thousand dollars or more. My son, who partnered with me in the construction business, was able to continue construction projects during my absence, which helped a great deal in keeping customers happy. Because I was a self-employed contractor, at least I didn't have to beg to be given a couple weeks of vacation time.

As the planning progressed, I found out we would stay in a seminary building during the first week, but the facilities would be much more primitive the second week. During that week, we would be camping out in tents in a cow pasture at the church construction site. Local church member members would cook our meals at the building site. Upon this news, I added tents, a sleeping bag, and an air mattress to my growing pile of gear. Bob Hepekoski, the Chilean missionary in charge of the projects, asked me to search for special self-tapping screws to fasten the sheet metal on the buildings that we would be erecting. We packed transformers since power in Chile was 240 volts at fifty cycles, unlike our 120-volt sixty-cycle current back home. Bob was skeptical that our battery powered drills would have the torque needed to drive screws, but we assured him he would be impressed. We packed additional power tools that threatened to drive the weight of our luggage over the seventy-pound limit. When the departure date arrived, my packed gear was just a few pounds over the weight limit. I planned to put some of the hardware purchased for construction in other members' luggage to spread the weight.

The mission team members from Echo totaled fourteen people. They drove for two hours, arriving at my home in South St. Paul, where they met my son and several of his friends.

We weighed items of luggage, made final adjustments, and marked all suitcases with colored duct tape to help in finding our bags when we got to our destination. We joined hands in a prayer for protection, safety, and good health and asked that the Lord would use us according to His will. My son and his friends graciously drove us to the airport and then drove the team members' vehicles back to my house where they could be parked during our time away. Doing it this way saved all the parking fees that would have accrued at the airport for the two weeks we would be gone.

After a Farewell meal together, we boarded our big jet and were swooped into the air. The flight time went fast as team members caught me up to date on what was happening in Echo in the fourteen years since I had moved away. We caught our connecting flight in Miami in an even bigger jet and were soon over the ocean.

Chile lies directly south of Miami but is on double daylight savings time year-round. This meant we did not have to change our watches and there would be no jet lag. I think they have double daylight savings because the Andes mountains bordering the east side of Chile block the morning sun.

Upon our arrival in Santiago, we were still tired from our long overnight flight. Being packed in the plane and trying to sleep in an upright position was difficult, and the best we could get was a couple of hours of cat napping. We were met at the airport by Chuck Ostley. Chuck, a missionary who originally came from Clarkfield, Minnesota, a town only a few miles from Echo, helped us speed through customs.

Because we had several hours to wait before our next flight to Temuco, we chose to walk around the capitol city of Santiago. Santiago had a population of about four million. At the time, the whole country of Chile had about sixteen million people. Half the population of Chile lived in a narrow fifty-mile-wide band that also contained the cities of Valparaíso and Viña del Mar. Santiago is inland about fifty miles from the ocean, but the other two cities are on the coast. Chile is less than one hundred and fifty miles wide but three thousand miles long.

We walked around the city looking at the old European style buildings and taking in the sights. We got to ride the modern underground subway to see the presidential palace at the center of town. It was shrouded in dark tarps and was being repaired from damage caused by the coup and ouster of the dictator, Pinochet, a few years previously. At the appointed time, we returned to the airport for our next flight.

I wondered what the airplane would be like for our short flight to Temuco. It was a local craft, but it was a jet. It had to be a 707 or something quite old. We heard a big thump when the craft went air born and rotated upward. I think the tail end must have bumped the runway. The flight south took less than an hour. When we landed at the small airport at Temuco, we saw the wreckage of a crashed plane along the runway. We were not sure when the crash occurred, but the remnants of the fuselage still sitting there didn't inspire much confidence. The landing was rough. We bounced about three times before the old jet settled into braking and came to a stop.

Bob Hepekoski and Sheryl Ottoson met us at the airport and had transportation arranged to take us to the old seminary building where we would spend our first week. It was a three-story structure built in the late 1800s. It had creaky wood floors and no elevator. We all had to carry our luggage to the third floor where we got our room assignments. There was a set of toilets and showers for us to use at the end of the hall. The gals had their own bathroom. The cooking was done on an old cook stove that was wood fired. The hot water for the whole building was heated in pipes that ran through the wood-fired cook stove, so the best time to take a shower was when someone was cooking.

Sheryl invited us to walk over to see her rented house, which was only one block away. The city of Temuco had a beautiful white stucco Alliance Church on the same street. The houses were all neatly kept and had either stone walls or iron fences around them. Most were painted with bright colors. We saw only a few with the earth tones that we see so often back home. There was lush foliage and many flower gardens. We saw palm trees with trunks that were three feet in diameter. Many of the plants and trees were unfamiliar to us. Sheryl's little house had everything she needed, even a garden where she showed off her flowers. She let us all use her computer to email to friends back home.

Later, we hiked back to the seminary for supper. An older gal named Dorothy served us. She was on vacation and was also a missionary. She offered to do our laundry each day and taught us some Spanish. She also helped cook, serve, and cleanup dishes. She just couldn't seem to sit still and enjoy her vacation. Later in the week, when we planned to go to Lago Ranco, she wanted to come along to visit friends there. We gladly included her in our group.

The next day, Bob took us out in the country to work on the first small chapel. The church was portable; that is, it could be disassembled and moved. The idea was that the building would be loaned to a starting congregation until they could afford a permanent structure, and then it would be dismantled and loaned out to another beginning church. The design was developed by a previous group, but they didn't have enough time to completely finish it. Our job was to finish assembling it and attach the sheet metal to the roof and wall panels. The whole building could be easily disassembled in only a few hours. All the panels could then be loaded on a truck and hauled to a new location.

We first built a wood floor consisting of eight sections that could be bolted together. Within several hours, the walls were bolted on and lagged to the floor. The walls were one-inch steel tubing with corrugated sheet metal on the outside and one-eighth-inch Masonite paneling on the inside. Then the roof panels went on. The whole process took five days. It rained the first three days that we worked. Only a few of us packed raincoats because Bob had said it was the dry season; the rest wore black garbage bags to try to stay dry.

The third day, the small building was finished, so we disassembled it and loaded it into an old grain truck. The church was going to be loaned to the Mapuchi Indians, and we were planning to erect it on a small plot of land several miles away in the heart of the Mapuchi farmland. An eighty-year-old Mapuchi grandmother was donating a plot of land for it to sit on. Her grandson asked us to take a picture of her in her best native costume, which he could keep. She was quite old, and he had no camera to preserve her memory for his  family. She, her grandson, and his wife and children lived a few hundred feet away in a small farm house.

The spot she gave for the church, though small, represented a pretty good-sized bite out of their small five-acre farm. We found that the Mapuchi land is similar to our Native American reservations. What they have is barely enough to survive. As families grow, their land is further subdivided between the children. This family was no different. They used every square inch for their crops, which were carefully tended. They farmed right up to the road and wasted nothing by eliminating ditches. Their animals were also well tended, and all looked like they could enter them in competition at a fair. They put collars around the necks of their pigs, using three sticks tied in a triangle with the crossed ends of the sticks projecting out. They explained that this stick collar prevents the free-range pigs from escaping through the fences. We thought they looked like "pigalopes," with their stick antlers.

When we arrived at the church site, several Mapuchi men were digging a hole for the outhouse. Others were trying to set up the concrete pylons that would hold the floor of the building off the ground. To get them level and positioned correctly, they used strings and a water level. The water level was a clear plastic hose about a half inch in diameter, which was filled with water. The hose was stretched out between pylons, and the water levels were compared, giving the correct height for the next pylon. It was a simple way to level things. Soon they had the twenty or so pylons positioned, and we unloaded the floor panels, setting them on the pylon foundation and bolting them together. We reassembled the building in just a few hours.

Pastor Sid, an itinerant preacher, came by to check the progress. He was an old Mapuchi Indian who was to be the pastor of this new church. He gave a long-spirited prayer, which was translated by Bob so we could understand. It was filled with thanks to the Lord and to us for providing him with a church building. He was so gratified that we would come from so far away at such great cost and give our time for construction. We were sweaty and muddy from crawling under the building after putting the bolts in the floor, and he was amazed that we would stoop to crawling in the mud to help them. We all had tears in our eyes when he finished his prayer. We didn't think the sixteen-by-twenty-foot church was that great looking of a building (it looked more like a glorified yard shed), but Sid was so happy to have a place to worship with his small flock of believers.

I offered to paint a small sign for over the door so that people would know it was a church. Bob asked Sid what he wanted to call the church

and what the sign should say. Sid said, I should paint "TEMPLO DE EVANGELISMO" on the sign. I sobbed as I painted the words, which meant, "Temple of Evangelism" on the small sign. Only minutes before, we had said among ourselves that the small building looked like a yard shed, but for Sid, it was God's temple, and he was going to use it to reach people for Jesus.

Each day after work was over, we would travel back to town and eat supper and relax. Often, we would hike about town looking at the gardens and the architecture. We discovered a city park a few blocks from the seminary, which had an ongoing flea market of hundreds of little booths tended by locals selling their crafts. They were open until eleven o'clock every night. It was a souvenir collector's heaven. It became our favorite place to go. I wondered if I was going to go over my weight limit again on the return trip because of all the souvenirs I had purchased.

Many of our team members were farmers, and they marveled at the size of the heads of wheat in the fields and the good condition of the farm animals. They used Sheryl–with her knowledge of Spanish–to converse with one of the local farmers as to how many bushels to the acre he got in yield and what wheat sold for in Chile. The answer came back in kilograms per hectare and pesos per kilo, so after doing a lot of math conversions, we found their yields were quite a bit more than we got back home. The wheat sold for five dollars per bushel, which is more than we get for wheat in Minnesota. The farmers in our team attributed the high yield and prices to the good volcanic soil and high demand for the product.

The farm family at the church location had been preparing a feast for us as we wrapped up the last day's work on the portable church. They had butchered several of their chickens and were making a big pot of soup. We had breads and jelly, watermelon, several kinds of vegetables, and beverages. When it started to rain, we moved our plank table on sawhorses into the chicken coop and continued to enjoy the meal and the company. The men passed around an old jug of some pretty stout apple cider. It had an apple core for a cork, and the liquid had a lot of floating bits and pieces in it, so I just took a small sample. Bjorn, Tom Ottoson's son, who was on the trip, asked if he could have some milk. It took about ten minutes for them to get him some, and it was warm. Later he found out that they had quickly milked their mare so he could have milk.

After the meal, we thanked our hosts and promised to come back for their first church service in one week. We said goodbyes and then air kissed all the women on the cheeks and shook hands with the men. The team traveled the narrow farm roads as we made our way back to the seminary.

At about four in the morning, almost everyone in our team came down with food poisoning. The illness kept nearly all of us vomiting and gave us diarrhea for two days. We never did find out what it was that made us ill, but we suspected the butchered chickens sat out too long in the sun. Also, preparing the food outside over a cooking fire in less than sanitary conditions had probably caused some salmonella bacteria to grow, causing the poisoning. We all recovered, but we were ill during most of the time we had planned to go touring before our next project.

We rented a Kia van, and that, along with the two missionaries' cars, gave us enough room for the team and all of our gear. We headed south and out of town for a several-hundred-mile drive to our next project. Our destination was the town of Lago Ranco, located on the shore of a large lake of the same name. The trip down was beautiful. We saw perhaps a dozen volcanoes on the way. The snow-capped Andes were always in our vision to the east. The roads were all blacktop or concrete. It was a pleasant trip, but we were not prepared for the beauty of the site where we were to build the next church.

After we traveled through the small town of Lago Ranco, we headed out to the church site. The Mapuchi congregation members had built an outhouse for us to use and erected a plastic and log shelter to serve as a kitchen and dining area. The church was to be located on the hillside out in the pasture. The congregation had already started laying part of the foundation.

Bob had sent money down to them several weeks before for materials for the church building project and was disappointed that there was no lumber there yet. He immediately got on his cell phone to find out when it was coming. We set up our tents in the cow pasture a couple hundred feet from the church foundation and prepared ourselves for camping  out. We blew up our air mattresses and rolled out our sleeping bags in the tents. Our view of the lake from our hillside was spectacular. We were perhaps five hundred feet above the water surface. We could see several islands out in the lake and the snow-capped Andes beyond to the east where the border of Argentina lay. The air was so clear that distances were deceiving. We found out that it was nearly forty miles to the far side of the lake even though it only looked like about eight or ten.

Several days later, we went down to the shore to swim and found that the lake was so wide that the curvature of the earth became apparent. Although we had been able to see the entire mountains from the tent site, they seemed to have half disappeared when we viewed them from the level of the lake. Cows, pigs, and horses grazed in the pasture. Hawks circled the  sky looking for mice. The fence line was loaded with blackberries and large red flowers–Chile's national flower. The Europeans introduced blackberries to Chile in the 1800s, but now they have spread throughout much of the country and are considered a pesky alien weed.

Several church members came out to the site. We met the Chilean carpenter who would direct us in their construction techniques. Another interesting fellow, who was a gun safety instructor, joined us. Through pantomime and use of drawings, we found out he loved to fish. His eyes got big when I said our northern pike could grow to over a meter in length. He promised to take several of us fishing the next evening.

Bob had found out that our lumber still had leaves, as the lumberjacks had not yet cut the trees down to have them sawed at a local sawmill. It wouldn't be delivered until the next morning. This timing setback gave Bob the opportunity to take us on a  tour to a park. It was on top of a 1500-foot-high flat-topped mountain that we could see looming above the lakeside town of Lago Ranco. We drove to the park and spent a delightful afternoon hiking several miles of trails and looking at large virgin growth forests. The park had a self-guiding nature trail, but all the signs that identified things were in Spanish. The vista over the small farms, lake, and the town was

 breathtaking. Some low clouds and banks of fog would occasionally block our view as they passed by at an altitude below us.

We headed back to our tent site late in the afternoon, where the cooks were preparing supper for us. In Chile, all of our meals– no matter how simple–were fussed over so that the presentation was appealing. Even a hot dog was made to look like an hors d'oeuvre. The Mapuchi women, who were cooking for us, served us fruit juices of many kinds, salads at nearly every meal, fresh baked bread (pan) and buns, and always fresh cut local nectarines. They ate much healthier meals in Chile than we do at home. The women were all slim and beautiful and took pride in their appearances. We had learned much from them about what constituted a healthy lifestyle.

The next morning, the fresh cut, wet lumber arrived. It was Eucalyptus but worked much like our pine, except it smelled faintly like the medicated ointment we rub on our chests for colds. Our team framed the floor much like the first church, but because this was a permanent structure, this one was not made in sections. The framework of floor joists that we laid out made a floor of about twenty feet by twenty-four feet. This building was to be a bit larger than the last small church.

The Chilean carpenters waste nothing in construction. I wondered why the Chilean foreman wanted to go to work on the walls before the flooring was put on the floor joists. He said it was important to get the building enclosed so that the interior could be worked on regardless of

weather conditions. He instructed us not to waste lumber using a bottom plate and explained that the vertical studs were to be nailed directly to the rim joists. The team sheeted the walls with zinc coated corrugated steel before they were stood up. Another part of our crew hand-built trusses for the roof while we worked on the walls. Within three days, the team had erected and weatherproofed the small church. We had to make the window frames by hand. Men from the church came out and measured what size glass to put in them. We had enough time to build a small porch and line up rocks on each side for a small flower garden.

We again painted a sign for above the door, identifying the building as a church of the Missionary Alliance. The tongue and groove flooring arrived but was way too green to fasten down because we knew it would shrink, so we just cut it to fit and laid it

over the joists. Later when it dried enough, the men of the church locked it together, adding a few more boards due to shrinkage, and finished the final fastening.

During many of the afternoons we worked, the temperature rose into the low nineties. We cautioned everyone on the team to drink lots of water so they wouldn't get dehydrated. Bjorn asked me how he would know if he were becoming dehydrated.

I replied, "If your pee is orange or brown, you aren't drinking nearly enough water."

He immediately made a trip to the outhouse. Several seconds later, the door flung open, and he ran in a panic to the nearest water jug and chugged down about a quart. We got a good chuckle out of him. Bjorn was a high energy person and was the life of the party. When his batteries ran down, he would just tip over and go to sleep for ten or fifteen minutes and then wake up and go full speed again. He spent quite a bit of time running his dad's new video camera and narrating the trip. We had six hours of video when the trip was over.

One afternoon, Tom Ottoson, Bjorn's dad, took the video camera and walked around interviewing each of us. He asked us what we thought about the trip. As I heard some of the others talking, I wondered what I could say that was meaningful.

When it was my turn, he asked, "What do you think we accomplished on the trip?" I was moved to paraphrase the scripture and said, "Sometimes we get to plow the ground, sometimes we get to plant the seed, and sometimes we get to bring in the harvest, but what I think we did was give them a tractor." Tom chuckled, as he understood what I meant. "The buildings we are helping erect are just tools for them to use to help spread the gospel. We won't see the harvest; we are just giving them the tools to help bring it in," I said.

About the third night we were there, the man who said he would take us fishing returned and drove a few of us about five miles around Lake Ranco to a spot where quite a large river ran out of the lake, heading to the Pacific Ocean about fifty miles away. He said it was a good spot for trout and salmon. I had taken a small collapsible pole and a few lures and was soon casting out into the rapids and retrieving back through the clear water over a deep hole. I had spotted some fish there, but we just couldn't get them to bite.

Our host was fishing with his string wrapped around a tin can. He would slip the can over his hand and twirl his lure over his head while releasing his thumb holding the line. It played out just like an open-faced fishing reel. He had quite a technique but caught no fish either. While we fished, a couple of jet skis and a large speedboat threaded their way up the rapids and made it to the lake. I was amazed they were able to make it through the rough and dangerous rapids.

One afternoon the girls in the group heard that there was a rodeo down the road, so they took time off to check it out. They were farm girls and loved horses. They had a good time and explained when they returned how the horses were trained to pin a calf against a fence so the cowboy could jump off and then throw it to the ground. This was different than our rodeos back home where calves had to be roped and then thrown and tied.

After construction was over, the congregation spread the word that the first service was to be held that Saturday night. People walked, rode bikes and motor cycles, trotted in on horses, and drove in cars to attend. I would guess there were over one hundred people, and all could not fit inside, so some stood outside the windows listening to the service. We had a building dedication service and sang many hymns and choruses. We got to participate in the service as well, with Bob and Sheryl translating. Afterward, we had a big feast of roast lamb and watermelon. We received many hugs, kisses, and thanks for building their church.

We sat around the campfire that night and reminisced. We turned in to our sleeping bags that night, tired but grateful for what the Lord had enabled us to do.

The next day, we drove back to Temuco and got to do our final shopping for souvenirs. Many of the team members had US dollars but were out of pesos which were needed for shopping, so I went to a booth that sold leather goods because I knew the man could speak some English. I held up a one hundred dollar bill and asked if he had pesos to exchange. Between his wallet, his wife's purse, and borrowing from the next booth, he came up with fifty thousand pesos. He eyed the fresh hundred-dollar bill I gave him in exchange and asked in a joking manner if I had printed it that day. Sheryl was surprised that I was able to round up pesos so the rest of the team members could shop for souvenirs, as the banks were not open.

Sunday morning dawned, and we drove out to the first portable church to participate in a dedication service for their building. Many people showed up again, arriving in every kind of vehicle and some on horseback. As poor as most of the congregation members were, many

carried cell phones. Chile had set up a series of towers, which ran the whole length of the long narrow country, and they had served to open up communications for the whole country. The cell phones were cheap there, so almost everyone had one. The service lasted several hours. We had snacks afterward, being careful of what we ate. We all wept because of the thankfulness of the people and the fact that our time in Chile was almost over.

Back at the seminary, we spent our last night and packed our bags for the long trip home. We again said tearful goodbyes to our Chilean friends as we boarded our jet for the flight home. We hated to leave this wonderful place and these friendly people, and yet, we were all a bit homesick as well. Upon returning home, we almost had to reintegrate back into society. It was almost depressing. We had a mountaintop experience and now were returning to the valley. All of us stated that we would love to go back.

Kiev, Ukraine

2001

Through the work of Paul Marty, a former member of our church who had gone into mission work, our church adopted a small congregation to help in the Ukraine. Paul, who had a thriving chiropractic practice, had gone on a mission trip there with his wife and had decided to make a big change in his life and go into full-time missionary work. He joined an organization called Hope International. This group provides small business loans to entrepreneurs in developing countries to help them start or build small businesses. It is a Christian-based organization. They raise money from various sources and then provide loans of up to five hundred dollars to individuals to help build capitalism. It has been very successful. They also help start kids' clubs that are Christian-based. Their work had been solely in the Ukraine, but they were looking at helping in other countries as well.

Paul and Cindy lived in the Ukraine by this time, and several other families from our church had joined in their effort. This led to our congregation to adopt the small Russian church. Eagan Hills Alliance Church planned a trip that would have up to thirty-five individuals–adults and youth–going to the Ukraine to help set up day camps for youth that would be much like our vacation Bible schools. I eagerly went to meetings with the group with every intention of going on the trip.

I began making cross kits, which consisted of two small pieces of wood that fit together in a notch to make a six-inch-high cross. Children could nail these to a base made of a small piece of plywood. The kit also had a small bag with pennies representing the thirty pieces of silver in the betrayal as well as two square nails and a piece of cloth representing Christ's passion and His robe. There was also a small die to show how the soldiers cast lots for His clothes. The children could assemble the kits and write the appropriate Bible verses on the plywood bases. It seemed simple, but our group wanted five hundred of them, so the volume of the unassembled parts filled several duffel bags.

As I was getting the kits ready, I thought I should also prepare myself for the trip. A month or so in advance of the departure, I found my passport and started gathering the things I thought I would need to take. I had a nagging cough that hurt, so I thought I would make a doctor appointment and get some meds for it. I planned to also ask if I needed any shots for the trip, and since it had been years since I had gotten a physical, I thought that would be a good idea as well. The trip to the doctor didn't turn out at all like I thought it would.

I thought I had a touch of bronchitis that was causing the pain when I coughed, but Beth, my general practitioner, said the x-rays showed my lungs were clear. She said because I smoked and my age, then fifty-nine, she recommended a stress test to check my heart. She scheduled me to have it done a couple days later at the heart wing of the hospital. At the test, I had struggled getting my heart rate up to what they wanted, but they were able to do an ultrasound before and after the exercise. I watched my beating heart on the screen and listened as the stress test administrator explained that the picture of my heart under stress showed that part of my heart was struggling to get enough oxygen. He said that I would be well advised to get an angiogram. He explained that they would put dye into my heart through a tube run into the vein in the groin. I still wasn't too concerned.

We scheduled the test, and a few days later, I reported to St. Joe's hospital where it was to be administered. I didn't realize I would be able to watch as the dye went through the arteries of my heart, but there it was on the screen. Then came the bad news; I had ninety-five percent blockage in one artery, ninety percent blockage in two others, and fifty percent in another one. My brother had a stent put in one of his arteries earlier in the year to open a blockage, so I assumed they could do the same for me. The heart specialist said, though, that stents have a twenty-five percent failure rate and that I needed bypass surgery.

Bypass surgery! That was major! How could I have such a serious problem without more symptoms? She said the blockages had been building for quite a while, as my heart had grown other arteries to try to take over for the blockages. She explained that what was going on is called collateral growth and that my heart could no longer heal itself. Surgery meant stopping the heart and taking a vein from my leg and quite a long recovery period. It meant that the trip to the Ukraine was not in my future that summer. She made an appointment for me to meet the heart surgeon. I walked out of the hospital with my head spinning.

The next day, I met the surgeon and asked all the usual questions. He acted as if the surgery was routine. When I asked how many don't get off the table, he said about two percent but that he had never lost a patient. I asked what would happen if I postponed or elected not to have the surgery. He said my days would be numbered, and it would only be a matter of time before a small clot would cause a heart attack. He said the usual hospital stay was five days and that I could go back to work within six weeks. He told me post-surgery problems were few but some people had swelling in the legs for a time until the body rerouted blood back to the heart. Others had problems with the breastbone healing properly where it has to be split to enter the chest.

Sensing my concerns, he stated that I should be thankful the problem was found before there was any damage to the heart and that my insurance would cover the costs completely. Without insurance, I would have had to come up with sixty-to-seventy-thousand dollars. He said the surgery could give me twenty or more years to live as long as I got my cholesterol under control and watched what I ate. He also recommended that I quit smoking. We scheduled the surgery for one week away. I left the office sensing my mortality. I prayed.

When I got home, I told my son and my friends and called my parents. Everyone stood by me and promised prayer. The prayer chain at church was notified. As the week went by, I took it a bit easier at work and spent evenings getting all the kits ready to go to the Ukraine. The day before the surgery, I was notified that it was postponed for a week and they would schedule for the following Friday morning.

When that morning came, I felt a calm but also some fear because I had never had major surgery, and this was about as major as one could get. They put me on a gurney and wheeled me into the operating room. My son, Matt; my brother, Paul; my niece Jana; and Parker, my renter, sat out in the waiting room. I was amazed by all the gadgets and machines in the operating room. The surgery started at 7:30 a.m., and I came to about 10:30 a.m.

Jana was amazed that I was coherent so quickly. She is a cardiac nurse and told the others I would be out until 1:00 p.m. or so. I tried to talk through all the tubes in my mouth but finally motioned for a pencil and paper. I wrote out a couple of questions about the surgery and found out all had gone well. They had done a triple bypass for the worst of the blockages. I didn't feel much pain. That came later when they removed the drain tubes from my chest.

Within hours, the nurses had me up and walking in place, and within a day, all tubes were removed. I was just to rest and get up and walk the halls several times a day. Soon, I was just down to Motrin for pain. The food was bland, but what variety could I expect with an all-liquid diet? It hurt a lot to cough or laugh, and heaven forbid if I had to sneeze. I knew that even when hugging a pillow to mitigate the pain, I would go down on my knees if I sneezed.

Lots of friends and people from church came to visit. On Wednesday, I got to go home. The first few days were tough. When Sunday came, I had Matt take me to church, as I wasn't supposed to drive for a month. We arrived late and sat down in the back when everyone was standing. Half way through his sermon, Pastor Bruce spotted me.

Astonished, he stopped his sermon and said, "Roy, what are you doing here?" "Listening to the sermon. Go on." He and the congregation were amazed that I was already up and about.

I could only stay away from work for about ten days and then insisted on going, as the soaps on TV couldn't hold my interest, and I had read every magazine and book I had. Matt made sure I didn't do much but supervise for a time, but within a week or so, I was doing light duty. Within a month, I felt nearly back to normal and had a lot more energy.

The church team soon left for Russia without me but were glad I was able to provide the kits. I loaned Megan, one of the team members, my wife's flute to play while she was on the trip. All I could do was stay behind and recuperate and support the team in prayer. After two long weeks, they returned filled with spirit and gave their testimony at church. I was moved to tears as the young teens recounted their experiences. There were few dry eyes that Sunday.

Megan returned the flute with gratitude. She loved to play but couldn't take her own instrument because of its great value. I knew Kathy was looking down from heaven, approving my loaning out her flute to Megan.

The group presented me with a carved commissar, a wooden statue made in the Ukraine. They said they felt the prayers coming from back home while they were there. All five hundred of the cross kits I had made had been given out to the children in the day camps, and they could have used even more of them. I was thankful that I had been at least able to participate in that way. I prayed a prayer of thanks also that I had my health back, and I expressed to the Lord that He continue to send opportunities for me to serve, and I trusted that He would.

Since the writing of this story, the Marty family has returned to the United States and are back in the church. Paul is in charge of Hope International.

Kathmandu, Nepal

2002

M arie Rose was the director of an organization called Child Hope. Marie and her husband, Dan, were active members of Eagan Hills Alliance Church in Eagan, Minnesota. Marie had worked with Child Hope for several years. This organization started with the discovery of great needs in the Asian country of Nepal. Silas Khadka, a Christian man from that mountainous third world country, had been starting Christian churches as well as orphanages to try to meet the desperate needs of his people.

I decided that I should research the area and learned that Nepal is most known for the Himalayan Mountains and Mount Everest (Sagarmatha in Nepalese). Nepal is a small country between Tibet and India and is about the size of Minnesota. It has, however, thirty-five million people who are crowded into many small villages and a few large cities, all of which are located in the small areas of flat land between the mountains. Kathmandu, the capital, has a teeming population of four million, but they are crowded into about twenty-square miles in a mountain valley.

Kathmandu's population is crowded into a land area about the size of the city of St Paul, Minnesota, which has only a little over two hundred thousand inhabitants. None of the buildings are over seven stories high because of the earthquake danger and the lack of structural steel for building. The average income is only about three hundred

U.S. dollars per year, and unemployment is high. In the capital and a few nearby cities, Child Hope supports nine orphanages with over one hundred children. The needs of this country are huge and Child Hope is helping do what it can.

Marie approached Paul and me one Sunday after church about the possibility of a mission trip to Nepal. She envisioned us going with her and another Child Hope board member and spending two weeks there. We would teach carpentry skills to unemployed Christian men from Silas's church. She said the men could use the skills we would teach them to make furniture for their homes or perhaps even start a small business. The ideas sounded intriguing to Paul and me, so we talked it over for a couple of weeks. We both felt this would be a good use of our carpentry skills. Paul had only been on one mission trip to Jamaica about ten years before and felt quite led to go. Marie and the other board member would be going to Nepal, regardless, to check on how the orphanages were faring. Paul and I would be able to tag along and benefit from their experiences from the numerous past trips they had made.

We agreed to go and began the process of raising funds. We wrote letters to friends, and the church took a special offering. One of my customers was moved to donate five hundred dollars when she heard about the needs. Paul was surprised to get a sizable gift from a vendor who did the carpet shampooing at his apartment complex. The money came in from numerous sources and was enough to cover all the trip expenses.

Marie said that our prospective class size would be eight men, although she was not aware of their level of experience. She said that with the funds, we would be available to buy each of the men a set of simple hand tools, lumber, and the supplies to complete assorted projects they might want for their homes. Paul and I felt we were going into this venture with little knowledge of what to expect. What we did know was that at least some of the students could converse in English, as it is taught as a second language in their schools. We gathered several books on furniture construction and put together a white board on which to make drawings to help explain to the students how to construct their projects. We each took some hand tools of our own to supplement what we would be buying.

We had no idea what Asian culture would be like but knew it would be quite different than the South and Central American trips we had made in the past. Nepal would not be as safe as other places we had gone because of the Maoist uprising that the government had been fighting for several years. Marie based us in Kathmandu where they had not yet had any trouble from the rebellion.

Our departure date arrived, and we boarded a wide body jet at Minneapolis-St Paul International Airport. The total air fare was over sixteen hundred dollars. Our flight would go directly to Tokyo, Japan. After a few hours' layover, we would fly to Bangkok, Thailand, and then board a flight to Kathmandu the next afternoon. The travel time would be about twenty-nine hours and cross twelve time zones. Marie planned for us to spend a day and a night in Bangkok to recover from jet lag. We settled into our long flight and dug into our carry-on baggage occasionally for crossword books, magazines, and novels to spend the time. It was hard to nap on the crowded flight, but we managed to get in a few Z's.

Many hours later, we landed in Tokyo, where Marie helped speed us through customs. After a short layover, we boarded another plane and took off for Bangkok. That flight was only about five hours long. There we met the other Child Hope board member, who had flown in from Denver, and we had supper at a nice hotel that Marie had stayed at on her previous trips. We were exhausted and turned in early, thankful to be able to sleep in a horizontal position.

The next day, we had time to do some sightseeing, so Paul and I ventured out and walked the streets as tourists. We marveled at all the street vendors selling produce and fruit that we had never seen before and couldn't identify. We saw beggars, many of whom where crippled or had serious health issues. One crippled woman pushed herself along, riding on a piece of plywood that had a wheel on each of the four corners. Another unfortunate fellow with elephantiasis begged along the sidewalk. Wheel chairs were a luxury in this country even though Thailand was considered wealthy by Asian standards. They had multistoried markets, filled with small shops. One could find almost any electronic gadget imagined, and nearly everyone had cell phones.

Traffic in the city was extremely heavy. Pedestrians dodged around taxies, motorcycles, bikes, and cars on the overloaded streets. Bangkok was low and flat and was crossed by many canals that also doubled as open sewers; I surmised by the smell. The canals were filled with narrow, speedy, one-hundred-foot-long canal boats, which hauled hundreds of people around the city. They must have been going about fifteen or twenty miles an hour down the narrow waterways. Paul and I walked around for several hours, always trying to keep our tall hotel in sight so we wouldn't get lost. Soon, however, we found ourselves in a ghetto on the wrong side of the canal, and we had to backtrack to find a bridge back across. We made our way back to the hotel, where we had a meal and packed up our belongings for the trip to the airport. There we boarded a Thai Air flight for the last leg of our trip. The Thai Air jet planes were the neatest and cleanest of any we had ridden on. They had great food and real dishes with metal silverware. The stewardesses were absolutely gorgeous, and most could speak English. It was a pleasure to travel this airline.

Several hours later, the pilot announced that we could see Mount Everest out the side windows. It was breathtaking. Several minutes later, we began our descent into the valley where Kathmandu is located. The smog was so thick that visibility was quite limited, but we could make out a city of small, densely packed buildings as we came in for a landing.

At the airport, we saw lots of soldiers with AK-47 rifles. Silas, the orphanage administrator, met us at the airport. He held the porters looking for handouts at bay and helped us get taxis for our trip to the hotel where we were to stay. Marie thought we would enjoy staying in Tamel, the tourist region of the city, for the first few days so that we could get in some shopping.

The trip to the hotel was an experience. In a city of four million, one would think that there would be more than a single stoplight. We rode around the city on the Chinese built blacktop highway that loops around the perimeter. We saw several machine

gun placements that were set up behind sandbags in case the Maoist attempted a coup.

There was no fast way to travel in Kathmandu. The rest of the roads were quite narrow and there was every possible type of vehicle imaginable. We saw thousands of taxis, buses, bicycles, trucks, rickshaws, motorcycles, motorbikes, and three-wheeled taxis called "Tuk-Tuks." Entrepreneurs had put every possible wheeled vehicle to use as taxis. To further complicate travel, our cab driver had to avoid the sacred cows that wandered all over the city and often blocked traffic. Our eyes burned from the smog, and visibility was only about a quarter mile.

After about an hour, we arrived at our hotel. It was a six-story structure about thirty-six feet wide on each side. The owner lived on the ground floor where there was a check-in desk and a small refrigerator full of bottled water. There was no elevator, and our rooms were on the fourth floor. We dragged our two 70-pound bags up the steps, and Paul and I settled into our room.

There were three rooms on each floor, and a room cost ten dollars per night. Marie had warned us to use only bottled water and to never drink the tap water or even brush our teeth with it. The bathroom was totally tiled, even the ceiling, and the shower spigot came out of the wall at the end. I guess the whole bathroom was the shower stall. After we freshened up, Marie took us out to eat.

We went to a restaurant called the Northfield Cafe. It featured a bar called the Jesse James bar. We had to believe that it must have been run by a Minnesotan, because Northfield, Minnesota, is where the James gang held up a bank, and they have a reenactment every year.

We sat outdoors in the covered patio because there was no air conditioning indoors. It is rare to find air conditioning in Nepal because electrical service is so sporadic. As we waited for our food, Paul noticed a large, perhaps three-pound rat scavenging crumbs beneath a nearby table. Marie let out a screech when I pointed it out, but Paul and I just took pictures of it. It soon left the premises, but Marie called the waiters over, and we told them about it. They didn't believe us until we showed them the digital camera picture of it. They then set out looking for it without success.

Finally, the food came. I couldn't eat my cheeseburger. I think it came right out of the freezer. It was a water buffalo burger since they believe cows are sacred in this largely Hindu country. It was burned on the outside and ice cold in the middle. The cheese was definitely not American but instead some sour, runny goat cheese, and the bacon had a boar meat smell to it. I've got a cast iron stomach, but it could not handle that. I settled for the French fries and a scoop of ice cream for dessert. Marie enjoyed her rice and vegetable dish full of mystery meat, and Paul picked away at what he had ordered.

Maric took us for a walk around Tamel. The streets were about fifteen feet wide, and there were no sidewalks. Taxis were everywhere. There were no rental cars available in Nepal–not that anyone would dare drive around in the horrible traffic, but at least taxis were cheap. Passengers could ride around for an hour for the American equivalent of a dollar or two. I don't see how they made any money.

Electric wires were all overhead, and it appeared as though if anyone wanted power, they just climbed a pole and hooked on. I saw no meters, so it must be a provided service, although power went off and on several times a day. I was amazed that there were not daily electrical fires from the maze of wires strung in all directions off the poles.

Marie showed us several internet stores where we could rent a computer for a couple hours and email home for just a few cents. I made use of that nearly every day, sending home numerous reports of our activities.

I was amazed at all the small shops. The average store was perhaps ten-by-ten feet. I saw few larger than that and many smaller. Each store had its own specialty; one store might sell wood carvings, another hats, and yet another incense. We even found one larger store that sold knives, which Nepal is famous for. There weren't any supermarkets, large lumberyards, or big hardware stores.

The next morning, we had breakfast at a German bakery and then hailed a taxi to begin the process of gathering supplies for our carpentry class. We found out our class now would have fifteen students, ranging in age from sixteen to fifty-seven. We located a hardware store, and Silas explained to the owner that we wanted fifteen sets of tools. We wanted to buy each student his own hammer, square, rasp, chalk line, hand drill, hand saw, drill bit set, chisel, file, and sharpening stone. The store owner's eyebrows went up as he realized the size of the sale he was about to make. He barked orders at a couple of young helpers, and they began climbing the shelves in the unorganized shop, looking for the requested items. He sent a runner to another store to get items that he didn't have or ran out of.

He owned a chain of three or four stores in various parts of the city. He had some English in his vocabulary, so we explained to him that we also wanted glue, nails, and screws for the students' projects. He did not sell nails or screws but said there were other small stores that sold those items.

The prices were cheap, and the budget also allowed us to get a few power tools for all to use. We looked at the limited selection and picked out a drill, a sabre saw, and a circular saw. They looked like the Makita brand that we had back home. We asked the store owner if these were the best ones to buy, and he shook his head no. He said these came from China, who made them to look like ours back home. It was the first of many cases of copyright or patent infringement that we saw. He showed us the same tools in a West German brand that we had never heard of and said these were the best tools he had. The tools were heavy and were wired to run on the 220-current that they have in Nepal. We boxed up all the tools and paid the owner, who was all smiles. It was probably the biggest sale he had made in a long time.

We had to go to another store for the screws because his store didn't carry the Philips head screws we wanted. Next, we ran out into the street and waved down a man driving by in a small empty pickup truck. We asked him if he was available for hire to haul lumber. He nodded yes, so we jumped into his truck and headed out looking for a lumberyard.

We found that the lumberyard was a large empty lot with an office building the size of a small shed. Their lumber stock was a series of jumbled piles of huge timbers of perhaps eight or ten different species of wood. We had to place our order, and then the owner said

he and his workers would cut what we wanted on a huge, old band saw. We said we wanted a bunch of one-by-eights, two-by-twos, and two-by-fours in pine. He said they would be ready in two hours. He sold no plywood, only boards, so we set out looking for a store that sold plywood. We found one a half mile away. We told the owner of that store, located in the basement of a big building, that we wanted to see what he sold. He had three grades of plywood: bad, worse, and totally unusable. The best was mahogany that had a lumber core that back home would have been much better quality and sold for about seventy dollars a sheet. In his store, it was twelve U.S. dollars and imported from India; we ordered twenty sheets. We had to pick through the pile. The lumber used in the core was often warped and when the mahogany skin was glued on and sanded, often the sander had gone right through the skin on the high spots, so the sheets would break as we picked them up. His helpers loaded the sheets we chose into our rented pickup. We then headed back to the lumberyard to pick up our boards, hoping they had finished cutting our order. Finally, the heavily loaded truck followed the taxi out to the orphanage where we were to hold our classes.

We had tied up the truck for nearly four hours, and when we asked him how much the bill for his services was, he replied, "Twenty-five hundred Rupees," which was equivalent to about five U.S. dollars. Back home it would have been at least ten times as much.

We unloaded the wood into a single garage adjoining the orphanage where our classes were to be held. The garage had a single light bulb and one outlet. Inside was a homemade table saw with a wood top. The guide fence had to be hand-clamped to the top. The top was made with two layers of plywood that were fastened together with a pair of hinges at the back side of the saw. To change the depth of cut, we simply lifted the top layer of plywood until less of the blade stuck through, and then we would put a wood block between the plywood layers. It worked, but then we were cutting downhill. There was no angle adjustment and no safety guards. There was also no electrical plug on the end of the cord, so we just stuck the wires into the 220-volt socket until it came on. There was no on/off switch either. It was serviceable but quite dangerous. We turned on the switch for the garage light, but it didn't come on. Silas said the power was off but that it usually didn't stay off long. After twenty minutes, the bulb came on, so we knew we could run the tools. About an hour later, the saw went off again for nearly forty-five minutes. Power was indeed sporadic.

Silas gave us a tour of the orphanage. It was a large, square, four-story brick house. The floors were made of marble. The orphanage was built for only twenty-two thousand U.S. dollars. Back in the states, a comparable structure would be close to three quarters of a million dollars.

On the first level was a kitchen, two bathrooms, a pantry, two bedrooms, and a living room with a fireplace. They had never used the fireplace because it doesn't get very cold. The bedrooms were full of bunk beds where the boys slept. The pantry had no shelves, but the food was in one hundred pound bags and piled high. There was a lot of rice. The kitchen had teak cabinets with marble counter tops and large sheets of grain-matched marble on the floor. It had a two-burner propane powered hot plate and a tiny refrigerator. There was also a small sink. One bathroom had a sink, toilet, and shower. The other had a strange toilet called a slit toilet, which was basically a hole in the floor that one crouched over while doing his or her job. I had never seen anything like that. Marie called them "squatty potties." The front room had a couch but little else. The whole house seemed nearly devoid of chairs, tables, nightstands, and dressers that one would have expected to see.

Minimal furniture was typical there. A house was basically a shelter from the elements and little more. The kitchen had a huge table with benches all around it where the children ate. The second floor was nearly a carbon copy of the first, but the girls stayed there. The third floor was Silas's apartment where he lived with his wife, Baktee, and his two boys, Veejay and David. On the fourth floor, there was an office and a large open area of flat roof that was used like a deck. On the roof of the office were two large, black plastic tanks that held maybe three hundred gallons of water each, which served as the water tower. The black tanks also heated the water from the sun.

The orphans ranged in age from about four to twenty-four. They were quiet, polite, and industrious. Many were doing their homework; some were cooking, and some were washing clothes. They all had jobs to do, and each had an older buddy to serve as a mentor. Some of them had come from small villages accessible only on hiking trails; many had never seen a car before coming to the orphanage. Some had lived on the street like wild animals, but they each had been taught to work cooperatively. They had to be taught to wash up and brush their teeth and how to use a toilet.

They had morning devotions with prayer, singing, and Bible study before setting off on foot for school. They wore uniforms to their schools. I was amazed by their good manners and good spirits. They had no toys but entertained themselves with  simple games and artwork. There was a large garden on the property, where they grew their fresh vegetables. The children were responsible for keeping the garden clear of weeds.

The orphanage had just acquired two Newfoundland puppies that the children played with. One of the pups was sick with Parvo. In the USA, the pup would probably have been put to sleep, as the disease is so often fatal. There, however, a veterinarian came every day and gave the dog injections and medicines. Later, when we got home, we heard the pup had survived and was thriving.

The only means of transportation the orphanage had was an old 250cc Honda Hero motorcycle. Silas thought nothing of piling his whole family on board and heading to the store for supplies. How they could  balance the kids and grocery bags on the rough dirt road back to the orphanage, I never understood.

Later in the morning, our carpentry students began to arrive. They each greeted us with a small bow and folded hands as if in prayer. About half of them could speak at least some English. Two of the students were from the orphanage, and one man named Abraham was Silas's oldest brother. The others were mostly from

Kathmandu, but some were from villages outside of town. Some were given money for taxi fare and for a place to stay while they took our class. Paul and I, feeling like we were winging it, decided the first thing to do was to build a couple of benches so that everyone had a place to sit.

The benches only took an hour or so to build. Next, using mostly power tools, we built a couple of sawhorses and set up a workbench. Other than hammers and tape measures, we had not broken out the hand tools yet. After we had the various benches set up, we designed a simple tool box, and all the students worked together to mass produce fifteen of them so that each could have one. Once these were all built, we divided up the hand tools amongst the students and had each person put his name on his box. This was all accomplished on day one of our class. The older orphans cooked for the students, and Baktee cooked for Paul and me. Paul and I commented on  how well the orphans had been trained to care for themselves and do their own cooking and laundry. Baktee explained how they taught the orphans these skills so that they could be independent. We asked about the facilities in the kitchen and wondered how they baked, as we saw no oven. Baktee showed us a small Dutch oven contraption that fit over one of the propane burners. It could only bake about an eight-inch-round cake. Paul wondered how they baked cookies and pies. Baktee asked, "What is pie?" Paul and I looked at each other and decided to do something about their primitive baking set up. Paul went out and hailed a taxi and then headed out for an appliance store.

Later he returned with a small portable electric oven he had purchased. I rounded up flour, brown sugar, apples, cinnamon, shortening, and a few other ingredients. We took over the kitchen as Baktee looked on with a very interested expression. As we got into the pie crust rolling process, she took half the dough and worked along beside us, copying what we were doing. As I cooked up the apples for the filling and the smell of cinnamon filled the air, she said she would try to make a filling of mangos. Soon we had two pies in the oven. I got to sample the apple, but the orphans made short work of the mango pie, and I didn't get to try it. I think Paul and I were a big hit with everyone.

We traveled back to our hotel that evening and spent some time walking around Tamel, looking at trinkets and souvenirs. If we showed any interest in an item at all, the shopkeepers grabbed us by the arms and started wheeling and dealing. They knew we had money and would do almost anything to make a sale.

I wanted to bring back some of the Kukura knives that Nepal is famous for, so we headed for the knife store. I bought about eight of the standard size knives as gifts for friends as well as a big twenty-four-inch one that was engraved. I also bought, for only sixty U.S. dollars, a forty-eight-inch sword that weighed at least twenty pounds. It is used for beheading water buffalo in preparation for butchering. I had no idea how I was going to get that back to the states on the plane. We stopped by an internet store, and I sent back an email to the people at church telling them of our adventures to date.

The next day, back at the orphanage, the students arrived, and we dedicated the day to making items for the orphanage. Together, we built  a large shelf full of cubbyholes for the kids to store their shoes and their book bags. We discovered that the orphanage had two kids sleeping on the floor because they didn't have enough beds. Several hours later, we had a sturdy plywood bunk bed constructed. The students spent some time sanding all the corners round. They seemed to be pretty pleased with what we had been able to build so far.

We told them to be thinking about what they would like to build for themselves because the next day they would have time to work on their own projects.

They looked through our books and were amazed by all the different kinds of tables, chairs, benches, hutches, and other furniture that could be built. Several picked tables for projects. One young man decided to build a hutch with two drawers for his kitchen. Another student, a twenty-one-year-old named Sam Pun, couldn't decide what to make. I asked him what he had dreamed of having in his home. He was married and had a small child about a year old. He said he had always wanted a bed but had never had one and had always slept on a mat on the floor. We helped him design a simple bed with a bookshelf in the headboard. Some students, those from out of town, would not be able to take a project home, so they asked if there was anything else they could make for the orphanage.

Paul looked at me and asked, "What about a playground? The kids have no toys and nothing to play on."

We put our heads together and drew up a quick sketch of a tower with a rope ladder, a beam with a swinging tire, another beam with rings, and two swings, and at the end, two teeter-totters.

We quickly consulted with Marie, who said money would be available for materials. Paul and I took the afternoon to go with another of Silas's brothers named Ek to look for materials. We traveled back to the lumberyard where the manager informed us that they had no cedar or green treated lumber. When we asked what would last the best outdoors, they pointed to a big pile of raw timbers. We ordered the boards in the sizes we needed. While they cut the boards, we set out in search of the nails, bolts, screws, chains, and hooks that we thought we would need for the job. We hired another truck and went back later for the posts and boards at the outside lumberyard.

Paul and I loaded the extremely heavy and hard boards. We suspected we would be drilling all the holes to fasten them together. We didn't know what kind of wood it was, only that it was the best kind to last outside. Ek came to visit a day later, and we learned that he was a forester. We asked him what kind of wood we had used to build the playground. He said it was teak. We had paid $7.20 (USD) per cubic foot for the wood. This comes out to be about $.65 per square foot. Back home you cannot purchase teak for less than $15 (USD) per square foot.

Back at the orphanage, we began the process of assembly from our simple drawings. The orphans watched attentively when they got home from school. They didn't understand what we were nailing together, only that it was for them. They had politely asked if they could pick up the bent nails and if they could have the scraps of wood we were throwing away. Some of them busied themselves making their own little projects.

Within a short time, the playground began to take shape. A blacksmith came out to the site to attach S-hooks to the chains for the swings. We had been unable to find any to purchase, so we had them made. The blacksmith came out and installed them for five U.S. dollars. When we were all done, we stood back and invited all the orphans standing on the sidelines to come and play. They looked at each other and then back to us with puzzled looks on their faces. Sadly, we realized

that they didn't know how to play on the playground we had built. Silas's father, a venerable old military man, stepped up and showed the kids how to swing and what to do on the teeter-totters. Soon the kids swarmed like ants over everything and were swinging on the tire and climbing the rope ladder and up the tower. They played for hours and didn't want to go in to eat.

Marie wanted us to get a good look at the Himalayas, so she took us to the airport so we could board a tourist flight on Saturday morning. We had our choice of two planes, Buddha Air or Mountain Air. We chose Mountain Air. Our flight cost $109 (USD) and would be for a couple of hours on a chartered turbo prop. The flight had two pilots and two stewardesses. The plane was small and could seat twenty-two, but there were only five of us on the flight.

We took off and climbed to twenty-four thousand feet and flew to the end of Nepal, where we turned and followed the Himalaya chain of mountains, staying about twenty miles away. The cloud deck was at fourteen thousand feet, so the peaks stuck up out of the clouds like large misshapen pyramids. The view was spectacular. The stewardesses came by and told us the names of the peaks as we passed them by. We saw K-2, Annapurna, and dozens of others. In a short time, we had seen seven of the ten highest mountains in the world. Then we saw Everest.

In Nepal, it is called Sagarmatha. It was breathtaking. The peak at twenty nine thousand feet was five thousand feet higher than the altitude we were flying. We found out later that fifty climbers had made it to the top that day for the largest number of  persons to scale the highest mountain in the world in one day. That was pretty amazing when one considers that one out of every twenty who had tried to climb it in the past had died. Most of the bodies are still up there and are frozen solid. At altitudes over twenty-two thousand feet, it is called the death zone and man cannot survive long above this elevation. The air is so thin that water boils at much lower temperatures, and the body starves for oxygen and water. Unless one gradually acclimates to the altitude over several weeks, a person would die within minutes if he or she were dropped on the peak by a helicopter. On the way back to the airport, the pilots invited Paul and me up to the cockpit to check out the instruments and see the view. This was before 9/11.

Marie and Silas took us on a tour of the city that afternoon. We got to see the main Hindu temple and the Buddhist temple. At the  Hindu temple, an open-air cremation was in progress, and the wind was in the wrong direction. It was an unpleasant smell–to say the least. One of the sacred monkeys tried to grab Paul's camera away from him, but Paul shooed him away. Then one tried to snatch Marie's purse. She let out a shriek, and a short-lived tug-o-war ensued, which she won.

The temple emitted a cold, creepy feeling and an overpowering smell of burning incense, which I will always associate with paganism. We saw a nearly naked, emaciated Hindu holy man who looked as though he was covered in ashes. Another was dressed in red and white and looked like a bizarre, frail Santa Claus. He held out his hand for some Rupees if one wanted to take his picture.

Next stop at the Buddhist temple, there were thousands of brightly colored cloths with writing on  them strung up all over. We found out they were prayer flags. They believed that elevating the flags covered with written prayers helped get the message to heaven sooner. Paul thought it looked more like a grand opening commonly seen for most retail establishments in the United States. It was an educational afternoon.

We also toured the old part of the city, where the buildings were over one thousand years old. Intricate carvings done in teak wood covered much of the exteriors. Upon closer examination, we were embarrassed  to discover that many of them were pornographic and depicted having intercourse in dozens of different positions. Many other carvings were of the thousands of gods the Hindus worship. We finished the day off with some more souvenir shopping and a meal at a restaurant.

On Sunday morning, we joined Silas as guests in their small Christian church. The church was hidden away down an alley in the middle of a block. It was not well advertised and there was no sign. At the time, only a small percentage of Nepal was Christian. We learned that there is freedom to worship whomever one wants but there is not freedom to evangelize. People were free to be whatever their fathers were but not free to try to convert others. Silas flirted with danger every time he baptized a new convert. Since our visit he has been forced to move to the United States to keep himself and his family safe.

In the church there was a pulpit but no chairs, benches, or pews. Men sat on mats on one side and women on mats on the other. The service had singing, preaching, and Bible readings but was not loud or jubilant. There was a sense that the church was almost running secretly. The experience gave us a better understanding of  how blessed we are back home, with our freedom to worship and our lack of persecution.

Marie announced that she was traveling to several outlying orphanages the next day and that Paul and I would have to find our own cab to get from Tamel to the suburb where the orphanage was. We arranged to have Amit ride the motorcycle from the orphanage to the main turnaround in the city to guide us the rest of the way. Our cab driver could speak a little English and understood where to take us. We hadn't paid much attention to the route and were now a bit worried that we would get ourselves lost.

On the way to our rendezvous point, we got in a traffic jam caused by crowds of Hindus worshiping around a strange looking, tall structure on wheels. It looked like a float at homecoming, except it was made of bundles of straw tied together. I asked the driver what it was, and he said it was a monument to the angry god.

I heard the words "Our God is a loving God come out of my mouth." He said "We have many gods here."

I said, "We have only one God." "I think maybe we have too many gods," he replied. I pondered his statement and was in complete agreement.

Soon we arrived at the turnaround, but there was no motorcycle there. We waited past the appointed time, and our driver waited with us, quizzing us about life in the USA. We shared some of our photos with him.

"Where do you need to go?" he asked, so we showed him on the map. He said he could easily find the place, so we hopped in and soon we saw some familiar landmarks. One of them was a granite ping-pong table with a row of bricks laid across for a net. Within minutes, we arrived at

the orphanage where Amit was just getting the motorcycle out to go get us. We discovered we had misunderstood the timing and had gotten there early.

We stayed the next few nights at the orphanage, as it was much easier than having to make the daily commute. During the next few days, we helped the students finish their projects.

One day, we saw a refrigerator going down the road. A man was carrying it home, using only a leather tumpline strap over his forehead. We witnessed why Nepalese men are noted for their short stature and for their strength and wiriness. The Sherpas from Nepal are famous the world over for their ability to carry huge loads up mountainsides and are in great demand for climbing expeditions. Seeing the man carrying a refrigerator down the road helped us understand the reason for their demand.

The monsoon season was beginning, so we had to string up a big blue tarp off the front of the garage to keep our students dry during some of the showers that hit during our classes. On one afternoon, one of the extensions cords we were using caught fire and totally melted, we must have been running too many power tools off a single cord. Despite the issues, we all worked on our projects. Sam finished his bed and disassembled it, hauling it home on his back in three trips. Another student finished his hutch and proudly showed us the two working drawers. All of the projects were rough, and we did not have enough time to get into painting or staining anything. In spite of this, Paul and I felt that the class was a big success and that we had given the students confidence and incentive to tackle additional projects on their own.

After the rain showers that evening, we enjoyed the air outside, now that it was washed free of smog. In the distance, up in the sky and above the cloud bank, two brilliant white triangles appeared. They almost looked like UFOs. It was the Himalayas! We were seeing them for the first time from the ground because the rain had cleared the air. We went up to the roof for a better look. Soon the orphans carried up benches and pillows for us to sit on. They were so considerate.

In the morning, I went outside to put on my shoes and one of the ten-year-old orphans said, "Uncle, wait." I waited and wondered. "I have something for you," he stated when he returned in a flash. In his hands he had a small stool he had built out of our throwaway scrap wood and discarded bent nails, which he had straightened. It had a small piece of carpet tacked on top for padding. He wanted me to sit on his little homemade stool rather than the cold concrete porch while I put on my shoes. I wept; I couldn't help it. I knew I was going to miss those kids.

That night, I went to both the boys' and girls' dorm rooms and spent a couple of hours showing them my photos from home and describing life in the USA. They had a lot of questions about my hunting and fishing pictures and couldn't understand why I needed to have so many vehicles or why I needed such a big house when I lived alone. You know, they had a point. They were all content with so much less. They threw a birthday party for me that night. The kids had all made cards out of scraps of paper they had scrounged up. Their art work was exquisite and colorful. I was getting used to being called "uncle." It was a term of endearment that they used when one had become their friend. I knew that I would treasure their cards and drawings and thanks until I died.

Our time in Nepal was at an end. After tearful goodbyes, we headed for the airport to await our Thai Air flight back to Bangkok. I was stopped in the airport by a soldier armed with an AK-47 rifle. He demanded to know what was in the long metal box. I had made it to carry the four foot-long sword I was taking home. I guess it looked like a gun case. I explained that it was one of the swords from the knife store that was used to behead water buffalo.

"Crazy American," he said. "Go on." This was the only trouble I had getting my sword home. We ran into Ek at the airport. He was going to an engineering conference in India. We waited together. His plane was late, and when it came in, we were glad we weren't flying Air India. It was filthy and covered with soot. Two attendants came out to change a flat with a hand jack. Pretty scary.

We made it to Bangkok and on to Tokyo, where Marie took a

different flight to go home to Montana for a family emergency. Paul and I had a nine-hour layover in the Tokyo airport. We slept, read, and walked around, but nothing was open in the middle of the night. Finally, our flight time came, and we made the last twelve-hour leg of the journey home.

Of all the trips the Lord has led me on, this one had the most powerful effect on my desire to continue to do missions work.

Antofagasta, Chile

2003

My friend and former high school student from my teaching days, Sheryl Ottoson, had been transferred from southern Chile to Antofagasta in the Northern part of Chile. Because she was working as a missionary for the Christian and Missionary Alliance Church, she had played a big part in getting a mission team to travel to Temuco, Chile, three years previously. She had been a missionary for over twenty years in the country and needed another team to come down to do work on an infant church in Antofagasta. A team from Echo, Minnesota, had arrived the year before to help with construction on the addition to the small church. Now they requested help from another team to put the finishing touches on the building. The biggest part of the job was to install a drop ceiling in the sanctuary and finish the electrical wiring.

This time the team was small, with only eight going. Most of them were from the Clarkfield, Minnesota, area. Four of those going had never been on a mission trip, and at least one of them had never been out of the country or on a jet before.

Our group leader was Kimm Jacobson, a veteran of numerous mission trips. Harvey Roepke, also a veteran of many trips, contributed skills of electrical wiring to the group. Ross Rieke, Kimm's brother-in-law, would be on his first trip. Todd Cole was a newcomer to missions and would be taking his college-age daughter, Melissa. Trish Bertek,

Melisa's friend, would also be going as well as Gordy Geisfeld, a veteran of one other trip to Chile. Our group, though small, soon developed a unique camaraderie at our organizational meetings, and plans went forward for the trip that would be in August. Fundraising began, and Pastor Carter Macfarlane of the Clarkfield Alliance Church gave good guidance in trip planning. The group had a mix of veterans and newcomers, and sharing past experiences helped the inexperienced in planning what to take along.

A month before our departure date, the National Geographic Magazine featured an article about the Atacama Desert of Northern Chile, which was just where we were going. We learned a great deal about the region that helped prepare us for the shock of the arid climate we were going to visit. We had no idea that the Atacama was the driest desert on the earth and that the city of Antofagasta had not had rain for thirteen years. Parts of the region had not received any rainfall in over five hundred years of recorded history. We read that when Antofagasta last had rain, it only amounted to about an inch, but over two hundred and twenty people died in mudslides that plowed through the middle of town late that night from the coastal hills above the city. Climate this dry is hard to fathom. The article explained that there are absolutely no plants in the Atacama unless they are watered religiously by residents. The hills above the city that rise over five hundred feet high are devoid of any plant life of any kind.

We also learned that there are few animals, birds, or bugs. All food and drinking water for the three hundred thousand residents of Antofagasta have to be imported into the city. The soil is rich but is rocky and dusty, and everything looks like a big gravel pit. The National Geographic pictures revealed a distinct lack of color to the landscape. It was all grays and browns. We read about the dry climate, but I am getting ahead of myself because we had not left yet for our trip and were not prepared for what we were to see once we were there.

In a few short weeks, the departure date arrived, and the mission team members assembled at my house in South Saint Paul, where we grabbed lunch and then set out for the airport. My son and some of his friends served as drivers to take us to the airport so the vehicles could be parked at my house while we were on the two-week trip, thus avoiding parking costs at the airport. Our luggage just barely made it under the weight restrictions, because I had packed a disassembled transit and tripod to help with hanging the drop ceiling as well as numerous hand tools that I had found useful on past trips. Soon we were winging our way south.

After a brief stopover and plane change in Atlanta, we were on our nonstop flight to Santiago, the Chilean capital. There we would change planes again to fly back north to Antofagasta. Napping, crossword puzzles, and a couple of novels helped the time go by fast. On the last leg of the flight, we watched as the land below became gray and brown and the last vestiges of plant life vanished in the dryness of the Atacama. We disembarked at the airport and were met by Sheryl Ottoson and Ruth Stover, another longtime Chilean missionary. They took us to a hotel where we spent our first night.

The next day we were taken to the church with all our luggage and were able to see the project we would be working on. We got to meet our host families with whom we would spend the next two weeks. Kimm and I got to stay with Nidia and Carlos Tejada, who lived right across the street from the church. They were a Catholic family that Sheryl had gotten to know while walking her dog in the mornings. They didn't go to the Alliance Church but were open to having guests stay with them. Nidia was a nutritionist, who had been educated in Spain, and Carlos was a psychiatrist. They had three children, Nicolas, Juan, and Monte, who graciously gave up their rooms so we could stay in their home. They also had a dog like most of the other families in Antofagasta. I think they all have pets because of the lack of wildlife in their part of the world.

Kimm and I had many interesting discussions with Nidia at breakfast each morning. She had a pretty good grasp of English as did Nicolas, her eldest boy. We found out that we could only drink bottled water, as naturally occurring arsenic poisoned the city water, which could only be used for bathing. Also, water and electricity were the biggest household expenses in their part of the world. Each morning, Nidia would supply us with fresh bread and pastries, cheeses and sandwich meat, and coffee and juice to drink, and we would talk about their lives and ours back home. We learned a lot about Chilean history and life in the desert. We found out that Antofagasta is a port city that ships out one third of the world's supply of copper, which is mined in the desert region.

After breakfast, we assembled at the church and began work on the ceiling. Even though our group was small, I knew that the ceiling project would probably be finished within a couple of days. I conferred with Sheryl and with Pastor Wilde from the church about other things we could work on. We made a list of additional projects, which included these items: framing and finishing a church office and three Sunday school rooms; building Sunday school and office furniture, including tables, benches, and bookcases; painting a sign for the church; painting the entire exterior of the building; leveling and packing the parking lot; painting all the windows, gates, and fences; repairing the pastor's kitchen cabinets; building mailboxes for the church and the missionaries homes; installing lights and outlets throughout the new addition; and repairing the baptistery.

It was a pretty tall order, but I thought we could get it all done if we kept at it and stayed organized. We dug into the work eagerly and were joined by several youths from the church as well as other church members.

Every couple of hours, the church women would call a halt to our work, and we would have a coffee break with pastries and fruits. We knew we would not be losing any weight on this trip because they fed us so well. Lunches and suppers were served at the church. The women chefs made even the simplest meals fancy. Tiring of the elaborate meals and hoping to give the cooks a bit of a break, we asked for just hot dogs. The gals served them up with pimentos stuck in the ends, which were cut and curled in a decorative way. The ketchup and mustard was put on in uniform squiggles, and there were several kinds of relish available. The layout included French fries (papas), napkins, and a fancy dessert. The presentation of the meal was everything to the Chileans.

Sheryl took me to the Construmart (the name of a hardware store) to buy materials for our projects. On the way, I asked her how she liked being assigned to Antofagasta after being in Temuco for so many years. She said at first she was a little depressed with the climate because Temuco had been such a lush green area of the country. But now that she has gotten used to the endless sunny days and gotten to know the people, she said she was content here. I wondered if I could ever adjust to such a change.

After arriving at the lumberyard, we bought Eucalyptus lumber, paint, and hardware supplies. I was surprised at the selection of tools and materials available. It wasn't like the large chain hardware and lumber stores in the states, but they had everything we needed at one store. We ordered the delivery of the sheet goods to arrive at the church that afternoon. We headed back to the church knowing that we had what we needed for most of the projects on our do list..

Within a couple of days, we had the grid framework for the ceiling installed, and Harvey hung all the light fixtures. They gave him fits because of bad ballasts in the fluorescent fixtures, and he had to keep changing them out. My transit proved invaluable in getting the ceiling leveled. Trish worked on priming the panel for a church sign, and Gordy worked on assembling tables and benches after our load of wood came. The church members were very encouraged by the progress and pitched in with nailing together the studs for the walls in the Sunday school rooms. By the end of the first week, we had made great progress.

Sheryl and Ruth said we should take a couple days off for sightseeing, so plans were made for a traveling trip into the desert. We hoped to see the big copper mine at Calama as well as the desert town of San Pedro. Sheryl and Ruth rented an additional car, and we all packed up small duffel bags for a couple nights travel and sightseeing. We left early the next morning and traveled on surprisingly good roads, heading north and east of Antofagasta, striking out into the heart of the Atacama Desert. Ruth wanted us to see the ruins of the old nitrate mining towns. After a couple hours driving, we were out in the middle of the desert when Ruth called a halt. We all got out and stretched, and it was then that we noticed it was a bit chilly, as it was winter where we were.

The first thing we noticed as we walked around was the silence, no sounds of birds or insects or anything. Just a deeply blue sky poised over endless expanses of gravel, with the road running away as far as we could see. There was no haze. Visibility was at least for one hundred miles. We could see the Andes Mountains far to the east. A little farther up the road, we came to a huge boulder where there was a sign designating the latitude of the Tropic of Capricorn. We left a sign there stating, "Wall Drug 8000 miles" with an arrow painted on it pointing north.

A bit later, we came to the ruins of a town just off the right side of road. The buildings had all been made of adobe, and the small amount of  wood used in their construction had long ago been salvaged for other things. The cemetery just outside of the city wall was huge. The graves were close together. The wood fences and crosses were all stained brown like rust from all the minerals in the soil.

From the late 1800s until about the Second World War, there were as many as three hundred thousand people living in hundreds of small towns like this one throughout the desert. They had come by the thousands after the discovery of nitrate minerals, which made excellent fertilizer and explosives. It was similar to the gold rushes that occurred back in the United States. They had hopes of getting rich by mining the naturally occurring nitrate minerals that crystallized in large formations all over the desert. For a time, some did get rich, but many thousands more died from the difficult climate and from being poisoned by the naturally occurring arsenic in the water. The graves attested to all who died. Each small mining town had thousands of graves. Many of the bodies had fallen victim to grave robbers and were missing their skulls. The bodies mummified rather than turned to skeletons because of the dry climate. Many of the graves were of small children who undoubtedly were more susceptible to the arsenic poisoning.

During the Second World War, Germany developed a process to make fertilizer and explosives from ammonia. Because they eventually could be manufactured artificially, the value of the natural nitrates fell, rendering a death blow to the mining in the region. All the towns fell to ruin, and everyone moved away. At one stop in our tour, we saw a number of abandoned locomotives, which had been used to transport the nitrates to the coast. They were all small and ran on narrow gauge track. Kimm was particularly interested in them and the roundhouse where the engines were spun around for the trip back to the coast. The trip to the mining towns was sad, but it was part of our education about the history of the region.

Next, we drove to Calama, which was home to thousands of miners of another kind. Copper mining grew to become a major industry. On the tour, we found out that Chile supplied one third of the world's copper, and we were about to visit the mine called Chuquicamata. Chuquicamata alone employed around twenty-seven thousand people and was enormous. We learned that the very large and deep open pit mine was a couple miles across and twenty-five hundred feet deep. Drivers of gigantic mine trucks hauled out the overburden and worthless rock out of the mine that they piled nearly one thousand feet high near the pit. The piles of rock had buried the original mining town and half of the second mining town that was built. Most of the miners had to move to Calama, located about five miles from the pit. We found out that it was cheaper for the mine to move the miners and build a new town than it would have been to haul the waste rock further away.

The mine ran twenty-four hours a day year round, and its fleet of giant trucks was something to behold. The newest trucks were the size

of a large two-story house and cost several million dollars each. The tires were sixteen feet tall and when the box was dumped, the top of the box was nearly seventy feet in the air. They could haul four hundred tons per load at a speed of two miles per hour. The back axle weighed nine tons and contained two huge electric motors that drove the truck. The motors got their power from a 2500 horsepower diesel engine that powered a huge electric generator. The trucks have automatic transmissions and to brake they shift into reverse and rev the motors. The driver sat over twenty feet in the air. They tended to lose a couple trucks a year when they slipped off the icy roads or backed up too close to the edge to dump their loads. The roads became icy at night because they had to be wet down to keep the dust at a safe level for visibility. At night in the winter, the daytime temperatures of sixty or seventy could plunge to the twenties in the very dry air.

Our tour guide was impressive. He took our bussed group into a room where a video explained the operation of the mine. Then he gave an explanatory talk first in Spanish, then English, then Portuguese, and finally in German. I think he knew a few other languages as well, but there were no other nationalities represented in our group except one man from Japan. The guide apologized that he did not know Japanese. He took us on a tour to the repair garage for the big trucks. We had to don steel-toed covers for our shoes and wear hardhats and lab coats. It was a fascinating visit.

He then took us to a scenic vista where we could look out over the mine and the refining facility. He explained that there are three different  types of copper ore mined, and each is refined in a different way. He stated that some of the ore is electroplated out in thin sheets, and the product is very pure. Another type of ore, he explained, is smelted with pure oxygen, which starts a self-sustaining two thousand-degree reaction that requires no fuel. The product is pure melted copper, which is poured into ingots weighing about five hundred pounds. A third process, he explained, involved settling out impurities and then further refining the product chemically. The settlings were then sold to other countries for nine thousand dollars per fifty gallon barrel. The waste contains a high content of gold, silver, platinum and other heavy metals. He stated that the refinery does not yet purify any metals other than copper and molybdenum and that molybdenum is used to make an extremely strong alloy of steel for things like drill bits and cutting tools. The mine was even going back to some of the tailing's piles and leaching out additional copper with acid. That process had been only recently discovered and was able to recover copper that previously was unable to be refined. The mine was safety conscious and had a good benefits program for the workers.

The tour guide pointed out the whip antennas on all the supervisors' pickups. "The orange flag on the antenna tip is so that the big trucks can see the small ones," he said.

Then, he explained how one time one of the big trucks ran over one of the small pickups because they hadn't raised their whip antenna, and the driver couldn't see them. Three supervisors were crushed, and the operator had to be flagged down because he didn't even feel the bump.

Back in the main square of Calama, we saw a steam-powered backhoe that had a bucket that could hold several parked cars. I asked why they weren't using it in the mine. He said the backhoe was one hundred years old and had been brought to Chile from Central America after digging the Panama Canal. He explained that it's just too small to be of much use now. I guess the diggers we saw from the viewing stand, which was several miles below, were much bigger than they seemed.

The guide said that within a few years the mine would be changed to an underground shaft mine because the cost of removing so much overburden of worthless rock to enlarge the base of the mine was becoming too great. The big trucks would still haul the ore out of the pit, but if it was brought up from underground, they wouldn't have to spend so much for fuel to remove waste rock. It seemed to make sense.

We left the mine and drove to the small desert town of San Pedro. It is a tourist town with a small Catholic university, a museum, and an open market. We found a hostel owned by a man from Switzerland, who spoke excellent English. He said he had visited the town and fallen in love with the area, so he opened the hostel and started a tour bus business. There were a lot of natural wonders to see near the town: Inca ruins, volcanoes, geysers, and a national park called The Valley of the Moon.

We spent the rest of the day shopping and managed a hurried visit to the Inca ruins just outside of town. The ruins covered a hillside next to a small stream. The stream came out of the high Andes and was fed by snowmelt. It allowed a ribbon of greenery to grow along its banks. There were small irrigation ditches controlled by gates, which rationed precious water to vegetable gardens and citrus groves. The produce was sold in the village. The ruins were stairways and rock walls that looked like they had been piled up recently.

We had to remind ourselves that there was no water erosion there. It hadn't rained in San Pedro in at least five hundred years, about when the Spanish conquistadors first arrived there. The Inca city must have had hundreds, if not more, inhabitants at one time. It was said this was as far south as the Inca empire extended. There, the Mapuchi Indians, a tribe the Incas could not defeat, stopped their expansion to the south.

Back in the town, we found an old Catholic church built in 1540. It was painted brilliant white and could hold perhaps one hundred people. The sparse use of wood in its construction showed the scarcity of trees. The boards of the ceiling were made of sawed up sections of saguaro cacti. The whole building was covered with adobe mud and whitewashed. The floor was wood and the aisles were worn nearly two inches deep by the traffic over the past five hundred years. This church was hundreds of years old before the United States was even a country.

We walked a few blocks away to a museum that was built by a Catholic priest who had been studying ancient mummies. He had recovered and carefully preserved many for display. The museum was part of the local university. It was interesting to learn the history of this area.

Back in the hostel, the owner said we could use the kitchen and to help ourselves to the food in the refrigerator and cupboards. He was going to leave with a busload of tourists, who he was taking to see the geysers. We assembled a supper and then entertained ourselves on his pool table and were able to send emails home on his computer. It seemed strange to see these amenities set up out in the open courtyard. We had to keep reminding ourselves that it doesn't rain in this part of Chile. Because of the temperature extremes between daytime and nighttime in the dry desert air the owner had set out extra blankets for us, but we didn't think we would need them. We were wrong.

In the morning, we made hot oatmeal and toast and sat out on the patio to eat. Within a couple minutes, we all headed to our rooms for jackets to ward off the cold. I glanced over at a water dish belonging to the owner's German Shepherd and saw that it was frozen solid. It was twenty-six degrees. The day before, we were running around in tee shirts! The dry desert air cooled quickly at night.

After breakfast we decided to split the team into two groups. Four went back to the Inca ruins to explore. I opted to go with the group to swim in the hot springs. Just outside of town was a park with a big swimming pool fed by hot springs. It was winter, but the idea of a swim in hot water sounded comforting. Upon arriving at the pool, we changed into our swim trunks in the bathhouse. We should have gotten a clue that this was not a facility to visit in the winter because no one else was at the park other than a couple of attendants. They looked at us like we weren't the brightest bulbs on the tree. It was thirty-two degrees, and we began to shiver. We climbed in the pool and were really disappointed because the water might have been eighty. It was not a steaming hot bath. It was like a swim in a chilly swimming pool. I took a quick dip and dried off, thinking I had had enough of that. I explored the park a bit and soon the others, beginning to turn blue, took my lead and climbed out as well. Back to town we went after our misadventure.

The rest of our group had not yet returned from exploring the ruins. Todd and Gordy told Ruth that they would like to hike up to the volcano that loomed into the skyline outside of town. The sky was a deep blue, and it was warming into a nice day. Ruth looked at him like he was nuts. "You want to hike over to the volcano?" she asked. "Yeah," Todd said. "We should be back in a couple of hours." Gordy was all for the idea and wanted to go with him. Ruth asked, "How far away do you think the volcano is?" Todd thought for a moment and replied, "Not over five miles." Ruth laughed and told him it was closer to fifty miles away. The clear air made distances totally deceiving. Unlike back home, there was no haze in the clear air to help us judge how far away landmarks were. Ruth pointed at the Andes Mountains in the other direction and said if we would drive less than one hundred miles through a mountain pass to the west into Bolivia, we would be in tropical rain forest. She explained that the prevailing wind in northern Chile is from the East. The moisture laden air blows out of the Amazon basin and as it rises up the eastern slope of the Andes it condenses and dumps all the moisture in the form of rain or snow and has nothing left by the time it crosses the peaks. Thus, the prevailing winds cause a rain forest to the East and the driest desert in the world to the West. It was a land of extremes to be sure.

After our mini vacation, we returned to Antofagasta to continue our work on the church. Trish and I made a number of mailboxes, one each for the church, Sheryl, Ruth, and Nidia, who lived across the street. "Usually," Sheryl said, "the mailman just throws the mail over the walls around the houses or pokes it through the gate. There is no danger of it

getting wet." Sheryl said she had missed paying some of her bills because her dog, "Bam Bam," ate the mail. We painted the boxes in red, white, and blue in the pattern of the Chilean flag, and we painted the word Correo (Spanish for mail) on them in case the

postman didn't know what they were for. We tackled many small projects over the next few days, doing lots of painting and detail work, which made the church look much nicer. We painted a bright sign for the front of the church and hung it up after we painted the whole exterior of the building.

One day, a driver of a big dump truck delivered gravel for the parking lot, so we rented a packer and spread it over the whole parking area and

packed it down. The next day when I came to church, I saw that the church mascot, a flea-bitten German Shepherd dog named Bob, had dug a great big hole about three feet in diameter in the fresh gravel to get down to some cool ground. The pastor

had arrived just ahead of me and was scolding the dog for messing up our work. One could learn a lot of Spanish just by reading signs, and I recalled seeing a roadside warning sign that said, "Excavación Profundo! Peligro!" I had surmised correctly that this meant "A deep (profound) hole! Danger!" because it was located next to a deep ditch that was being dug for some storm sewer piping.

The pastor knew no English at all, so I pointed to the hole Bob had dug and stated, "Excavación profundo!"

He said, "Si, Si," then looked at me like a miracle had happened and all of a sudden I could speak Spanish. I had to assure him it was not so by saying, "No comprendo," to his excited babbling in Spanish.

We found that Spanish could be pretty easy to learn because the vowel sounds are always the same. I learned quite a few words and phrases in just a short time because being immersed where Spanish was the primary language forced one to use it.

In the afternoon, we opened up a hatch in the floor, which led to a below floor baptismal tank. We cleaned it out and caulked it to stop the leaks. The inside walls of the church got a coat of paint as well. Then we started work on the pastor's house, fixing drawers and cupboard doors. We re-glued a bunch of his chairs and the kitchen table, then did some painting on the outside of the parsonage, which was right next to the church. The effects of salt in the sand with which the stucco is made and the salt carried inland by the fog off the ocean often damages the paint. We coated most of the walls with "pasta," a pasty undercoating which we troweled on

before we painted to minimize the effects of the salt.

One afternoon, one of the church elders invited me to go fishing with him. I had taken a cheap telescoping rod along with me on the trip just in case. We headed for the ocean, and I could see he had a small packsack and a handsaw. I didn't know why he had the saw, but I thought I would learn why soon enough. When we got to the volcanic rocks near the shore, he climbed down and sawed off a bunch of barnacles. He dug out the bright orange meat and motioned to put it on the hooks for bait. He fished with some white string, a hook, a large nut for a sinker, and a tin can. He wrapped about seventy-five feet of string around the tin can until he got close to his hook and sinker. He stuck his left hand into the open end of the can and swung the sinker around over his head like a lasso and then let it fly toward the ocean. The line spooled off the tin can just as nicely as my fifty dollar fishing reel. Soon after he released his line, he wound it back in, and within a couple of casts, he had about a two-pound fish caught on barnacle meat for bait. I was still trying to set up my rod. He continued casting and caught another fish about the same size. I cast out and snagged a rock, losing my hook and sinker. I tied on another hook and sinker. My second cast had the same result. After losing about eight sinkers and hooks, I just watched him fish. He yelled something at me and grabbed my sweater and camera and  quickly backed up. I wondered what he was trying to tell me and then turned around to see a big rogue wave coming in, which got me soaking wet and almost knocked me off my feet. It was a fun time, but I realized I had a lot to learn about fishing techniques in the ocean

Chileans love to party, and Todd's daughter, Melissa, had a birthday while we were there, so we decorated our lunchroom with signs, balloons,  and crepe paper. Then we shared a cake and some ice cream and sang happy birthday to her.

Before we knew it, we were out of work and out of time, so we packed up our tools and headed for home. The congregation gave us small tokens of appreciation, and we shared gifts of hats and candy with the parishioners and their kids. We sadly said our goodbyes and all too soon, we were back on our plane heading to the big airport in Santiago, where we would catch our overnight flight back home. It was a time to thank the Lord for the friends we made and the work He allowed us to do. We were grateful for the hospitality of the Chileans and the special enjoyment of our mini vacation to the desert and the big copper mine.

Reñaca, Chile

2005

In the late fall of 2004, I got a phone call from Kimm Jacobson, a member of the Clarkfield New Life Alliance Church. He had led our last Chile mission trip to Antofagasta in the desert of northern Chile in 2003.

He asked, "Are you ready to go to Chile again?" "Sure. Where and when?" I asked. He replied, "The Clarkfield church is planning another trip. We are starting to put together a group to go to Viña del Mar in central Chile."

He explained that the local missionaries there, Chuck and Betty Ostley, were originally from the Clarkfield church, and they had asked for a team to come and help in the construction of a new Alliance Church in the suburb of Reñaca.

Reñaca is adjacent to the cities of Viña del Mar (pronounced Veena dale Mar) and Valparaíso (pronounced 'Bal-puh-ray-soh') and is right on the Pacific coast. They are about fifty miles from the capital city of Santiago and lie in a fifty-mile-wide band across central Chile. Half of the sixteen million people in Chile live in this band.

Pastor Carter scheduled a preliminary meeting. I mentioned the trip to my young friend Jesse Krech, who had recently rededicated his life to the Lord. Jesse worked for me in construction and had been on the Paraguay trip nine years before, in 1994, when he was a teenager. His dad, Jim, had taken him along on that trip to let him experience mission work. It did not take much talking to convince Jesse that he ought to go.

At first, the plans were for two groups to travel to Chile. One group would go to Antofagasta in the desert north of Chile and continue work on the church there, and the other group would go to work with the Ostley's in Reñaca. I was hoping to go back to the desert area with Jesse and see the progress on the Antofagasta church. Through emails, calls, and letters we learned over the next few weeks that God's timing was not right for a trip to Antofagasta. Sheryl Ottoson was the missionary there, and she said that the plans for that church's expansion were still in the infancy planning stages and that as much as she would like to have a group travel there, it would not be as fruitful as we had hoped. Instead, a group from her home church in Echo, Minnesota, consisting of her parents, sister, and brother would travel with us to Santiago and then travel up just to visit her.

A few weeks later, Jesse and I drove together to the Clarkfield church for an initial meeting. Clarkfield is about one hundred and fifty miles due west of the Twin Cities. We took in their Sunday service and helped ourselves to heaping plates of a hot dish at the potluck afterward. We got to meet Carter McFarlane, the pastor, and all the people who were interested in going. Plans for the group were spelled out. We discussed the dates we would go and the costs of the airfare. We planned to stay with local church members' families in Chile. Altogether, the trip would cost in the neighborhood of sixteen hundred dollars each, and we would be gone fifteen days. Seventeen people were planning to go, and Kimm Jacobson would again serve as the group leader. It was a sizeable group, which was made up of about one-third Clarkfield church members

A couple, Herb and Annie Siemen, from Fargo, who were former members of a church the Ostleys had pastored in North Dakota, planned to join us. One young man named Tim from Hibbing and a young teenaged girl named Kelsey from Rochester were also part of the group. Another couple who joined us was Gary and Marilyn Jacobson from Roseville, and we also had Byron Higgens, a newspaper owner, from Grantsburg, Wisconsin, in the group. Robert from Vesta, Minnesota, also signed up to go. A bilingual Hispanic couple from nearby Hanley Falls, Minnesota, volunteered and turned out to be invaluable as interpreters on the trip. Aaron Rupp from Minneapolis rounded out the team. This would be the first mission trip for many on the team.

Some of the ladies would serve as cooks for the group. Byron and Aaron would serve as historians whose job would be to record the whole trip in pictures and words that would be given to us at the end. It was an interesting group with ages ranging from fifteen up to sixty-five. Kimm worried that such a large group might be ungainly, but we trusted in the Lord for everyone to have a good experience. Carter and Kimm set dates for a couple more planning meetings and for the deadlines to get our funds raised. Jesse and I drove home excited by the plans for the trip and the prospects of serving the Lord. Eagan Hills Alliance had a special offering the following Sunday that helped a great deal with the funds that Jesse and I needed to raise.

As the time for departure neared, I began packing my bags. We were allowed two 70-pound pieces of luggage and a forty-pound carry-on. As I gathered together all the tools and supplies, I knew I would be well over the weight limit. I had over fifty pounds of nails and screws alone for the two pneumatic nail guns I planned to take. I packed up my luggage and ran the weights of my duffle bags up to sixty-eight pounds on the bathroom scale. The rest would have to be carried by others in the group whose suitcases weren't so close to the weight limits.

On the appointed departure day, the team members arrived at my house in South Saint Paul several hours before the flight time. As we had arranged for past trips, my son and several of his friends agreed to drive us to the airport and then take everyone's vehicles back to my house to be parked there while we were gone to avoid the expense of airport parking. I found room for my overweight items in other members' luggage and gave everyone a quick tour of my house, which was undergoing a major addition. We loaded up and took off for a large buffet-style restaurant where we had our sendoff meal together.

Soon after we arrived at the airport, where we met some of the other group members who had elected to drive directly there. We counted noses and checked that everyone had their passports and travel documents. We said goodbye to my son and his friends and got in line for check in and for getting our tickets. With all our tools, nails, screws, and assorted iron, we ran into a bit of grief getting through the magnets and x-ray equipment. After a brief baggage inspection, we made it through and headed to our gate, then sat down to wait for our flight to load

Soon we were all aboard and our plane took off for Atlanta, where we would board our international flight to Santiago. Our team huddled and prayed for no delays and safety and everyone's health. We were not plagued with missed flights as one of the past teams from Echo, Minnesota, had been. After a short wait in Atlanta, we boarded our big jet for the long overnight leg of the flight to Chile. We passed the time reading, visiting, napping, watching movies, and doing crosswords. I got to know several of the team members much better during those hours and knew that this trip was going to be great.

When we landed in Santiago, the team was met by Sheryl Ottoson, Bob Hepakoski, Betty and Chuck Ostley, and one other missionary based in Santiago. It was great for us to see them all again. They helped load our luggage on a bus, which was provided by Raoul, one of the Reñaca church members, who owned a tour bus company. The bus had enough seating, but when all our luggage was packed aboard, it was really overloaded weight wise

We said goodbye to Sheryl and her family members at the airport as they left to board a flight back north to Antofagasta. Together with the Ostleys, we left on the bus to make the fifty-mile trip to Reñaca, on the Pacific coast. Raoul entertained us by leading us in singing "Home on the Range" and other songs in his curious Spanglish accent. Halfway to Reñaca, the bus blew out one of the back dual tires. Raoul said, "One tire–not to worry; two tires–then we have problem.

Soon the driver found a small gas station and a deal was struck to change the tire. We wandered around and purchased sodas and snacks until the station attendant replaced the tire. Back on the bus, we crested a hill and had a beautiful view of the fourteen-mile-long coastline of the harbor. Valparaíso blended right into the suburbs of Viña del Mar and Reñaca in the arch of the hills. Street signs were the only way to tell we were in a different city. We learned that several hundred thousand people lived in Valparaiso and its suburbs.

Valparaíso is one of the biggest deep-water ports in the world, and they had huge facilities for loading container ships. The harbor had a gigantic derrick and crane system that was several hundred feet long and over a hundred feet high. It was assembled in Holland and shipped there by barge. The large harbor and the city that crept up the hillside was a beautiful sight. Our driver skillfully piloted the bus down the coastline highway through the city in heavy traffic, which was heading to the north side suburb, Reñaca. Within a short distance, we turned away from the ocean, drove inland several blocks, and arrived at the church construction site, where we would be meeting our host families.

The church site was kind of a shock at first. The lot was only about an acre and a half of mostly steep hillside. The unfinished building looked like two large, stacked grey concrete boxes jammed into the hillside with a long handicap access ramp leading up to the second floor. The parking lot was gravel, and the whole site was  surrounded by a six-foot-tall chain link fence. The red, rocky dirt of the hill lay exposed in the extensive excavation they had done to burrow the church structure into the hillside. We walked around, getting acquainted with the people and the building that we would spend the next two weeks working on. It looked pretty rough. I met Pastor German (Pronounced er mahn) Vasquez and his wife Nadia and their little girl, Isadora. Harvey and I were assigned to stay with them. They lived in a rented house, only six or eight blocks up the hill from the church

We loaded our luggage into his tiny car and found that he would have to make two trips to get us to his house. Almost everyone in Chile drives tiny two-to-four-cylinder cars because a large car with poor mileage would be way too expensive to drive. Chile imports all its oil therefore gasoline costs over five U.S. dollars per gallon. It didn't take long for everything to be shuttled up the hill to his little stucco house

Nadia said, "Our casa (house) is your casa." She could speak very good English, but German could not. They were so cordial and friendly that I almost got a lump in my throat. They gave each of us our own rooms and showed us how to work the wall heater for hot water for showers. They let us use their computer to email home the information that we had arrived safely. Isadora took to us right away and climbed up on our laps. She had long black hair and dark brown eyes and a 500-watt smile

Nadia made us some sandwiches with pan, a Chilean bread, and we sat down to eat. We plied each other with questions about what it was like living in our respective countries. We got out our pictures and shared a bit of America with them. We found German could understand a good deal of what we said even though he did not speak English. Nadia gave us the first of many lessons in speaking Spanish. The most important thing we learned was that all the vowels have only one sound in Spanish. A is always ah, E is a long A sound, I is a long E sound, O is a long O, and U is an OO sound as is raccoon. This helped a lot in pronouncing Spanish words. At grace over the meal, German prayed for a miracle that we would soon speak their language. He had a great sense of humor, which became even more evident in the subsequent days.

In the morning, Nadia made a simple breakfast of sandwiches, juice, and coffee. I was already missing my Mountain Dew, my usual breakfast fare, but I knew I would have to get over my craving or learn to like an alternate soft drink because my brand of choice was not sold in Chile

After breakfast, Harvey and I packed ourselves and our tools into German's tiny car and rocketed down the hill to the church. We were two of the first to arrive, as we had the shortest distance to travel. Soon the others were dropped off by their host families. We had our first devotional and prayed for safety, good fellowship, health, and a productive day.

We met with Chuck Ostley, the resident missionary, who outlined what needed to be done the first day. We expressed several concerns such as lack of a baño (toilet), and he said he would get right on it. We requested building materials and tables and chairs for the group, as we would be eating lunches at the building site. After Chuck left to take care of our needs and order materials, we met with Kimm for assignments for work

It was decided that we would first build benches and tables so the group could use them for devotions and meals at the site. Next, we would build scaffolding and ladders to work on the high places and the drop ceiling that was to be installed. Harvey, the faithful electrician,  went right to work to get us power and lights. Within hours, we had two 8-foot tables and four benches built for the group to use. Some of the church members had taken time off work to help with the building projects. They seemed to be encouraged by how fast we were able to build things. The team was divided into several groups that each had their own projects to work on

As soon as the furniture was built, we went to work on the downstairs to build a temporary storage room in the corner, with a locking door so that we could leave our tools on site. In Chile, instead of two-by-fours, they build with full-cut two-by-threes made of eucalyptus wood. The wood was easily worked and cuts easily like poplar or soft white pine. Before long, a six-foot-by-twelve-foot bodega (storeroom or closet) with shelves for tools was walled off, and the sheetrock was going up.

Herb and his team of helpers coated the entire downstairs ceiling with a paste. In Chile, workers coat nearly every painted surface with a paste-like material that is similar to a ceramic tile adhesive. The material prevents the paint from blistering and corrosion from the salt-laden air coming in from the ocean. The team took all day to coat the ceiling, but when they were done, the dingy gray concrete looked like white stucco, as they had swirled the  paste to create the stucco look. They planned to paint the ceiling the next day and then repeat the process on all the downstairs walls.

It seemed every two hours or so it was coffee time. The team of gals did a marvelous job providing sandwiches, fruit, pastries, tea, coffee, and juice for all the workers. Another team painted all the benches and tables we had built so they would be easier to clean and look nice

Ben, the teenage son of one of the congregation members, who could only speak a little English, tried to ask me something and then stopped and said, "Wait!" He ran to his dad to find out how to word his question and then came back. He asked in very correct English, "How can I assist you?"

I chuckled at his question and that he tried so hard to ask it the correct way. I also enjoyed how eager he was to help, so I put him on the random orbit sander and showed him how to sand all the edges of the furniture so no one would get slivers. He loved being able to help and felt important that he got to run a power tool

Lunch was an extravaganza, and we had to caution the gals that if we kept eating like this, we would all gain weight. We voted for simpler fare. Bathrooms continued to be a problem, as the biffy took two days to arrive. Prior to its arrival, we had to continually run to the woods across the road to take care of business or run down the block to the gas station

As the day came to a close, we felt much had been accomplished, and plans were made for the next day's work. We met Andre, who had been hired to be the night watchman to guard the site and our tools. He was an interesting young man, who was married and going to school. I lent him a book of short stories I had written about my adventures in the canoe country of northern Minnesota. He was elated. Our families arrived to give each of us rides to our respective hosts' homes.

At German and Nadia's, we stayed up late talking and sent emails home about the first day's adventures. We took showers and learned that if the volume of water is turned down low, the water is much hotter. It felt great to wash off the grime from our work. We slept like logs and awoke refreshed to the smell of hot coffee. We were beginning to pick up a little Spanish and tried to speak it as much as possible. After finishing our coffee, we piled into German's little Mazda and raced down the hill.

White knuckled during the ride down the hill, I asked German, "Terminal velocidad?" He replied, "Si," with a grin and didn't slow up a bit even though he could see I was a bit concerned by how fast he drove. We made it safely and began another day's work.

More lumber had been delivered, so we began to layout the walls for the two bathrooms and the kitchen. Kimm's team attached eyelets into the concrete ceiling and connected wires to them to suspend the grid for the drop ceiling. They had used my laser level to get the correct height and a chalk line to layout the lines for the eyes.

Even more helpers from the church showed up along with many of Julae's schoolmates. Julae is the daughter of Chuck and Betty Ostley, the missionaries in Reñaca. Betty scolded her daughter for skipping classes to help us. Julae was a straight A high school student. I helped her on a couple of nights with her chemistry homework. The beautiful teenage Chilean girls proved to be a bit of a distraction for some of the team members, but they contributed much to the work of the project.

As the day progressed, we finished framing the rest of the walls, and the sheet rockers took over. Another team began putting hinges and locks on the four doors that we needed.

When we had arrived at the building site, none of the doors and windows had been installed yet. We discovered that the contractor who had done the concrete work was a bit sloppy and none of the window openings was square, so a team of Chilean contractors came and set forms inside of the jambs to square up the openings. We also found that the poured concrete ceiling sagged about three inches and that it allowed water to puddle on the temporary roof, which then slowly dripped through. Therefore, we could not set the ceiling tiles in the metal grid until the concrete above was waterproofed or corrected somehow

The paste and paint teams finished up the big downstairs room and made plans to begin the upstairs the next day. Chuck was kept busy running to the Construmart (big lumber yard) for materials, so we didn't see him much during the day. We made plans to paint a big sign for the church; therefore, we ordered plywood and paint for him to pick up.

On the way home that day, German stopped at a local gas station, and we were again amazed at how expensive gas was. German was on a tight budget and didn't even fill up the six-gallon tank. At home that night I broke out more pictures and showed Nadia photos of the diamond willow furniture that I make back home

German pointed to the pictures and said, "muebles rustico" (furniture that is rustic). Nadia requested, "If you have time, could you make a small chair for my daughter, Isadora?" I said I would. Then, I gave them the Scrabble game I had brought for a gift, and we had a fun night playing Scrabble in Spanish and English. German again prayed for a miracle that we would somehow learn Spanish. We thoroughly enjoyed visiting with our hosts but finally had to turn in and try to catch up on some sleep.

In the morning, German was busy, so Nadia had to take us down the hill in the car. German indicated that we should be sure to wear our seat belts because Nadia was a less experienced driver. He said, "Uno momento," (one moment) then ran back in the house to get us some bicycle helmets to wear "for safety," he said

We knew he was only joking. Actually, I felt safer with her because she didn't speed. At the church, I got to talk to Andre, who stayed for our devotional. Each morning the devotions featured a different team member who would give a testimony or a Bible passage with special meaning, and we would sing a few choruses followed by prayer. Andre, who spoke very good English, talked to me at length about my book of stories and asked lots of questions about life in America. He was Catholic and was curious about the Christian and Missionary Alliance. I told him a lot about our church. Then it was time to get to work, so we began to layout the tile floor for the downstairs. We had a daunting task ahead of us. We had about twenty-five hundred square feet of tile to install, but the concrete substrate was rough and crumbly. Choosing the cheapest bid for the concrete work had resulted in the contractor skimping on the Portland cement in the mix making for very weak, rough concrete

We set up our lines to follow and began mixing the thinset mortar we would use to stick the tile to the floor. It was applied with a trowel with big notches to make the mortar stand up and bridge the rough spots. Most of the tile products don't contain a latex additive, so the thinset was not as sticky as I was used to in my contracting work back in Minnesota. We found in subsequent days that many of the tiles didn't stick well, and we had to pull up over one hundred of them and reset them. The sheetrock crew had finished hanging the sheetrock panels and began to do the taping to cover the nail heads and seams.

The ceiling crew began hanging the metal grid that would hold the acoustic ceiling panels, and Harvey fastened in the plastic conduit for electricity to the lights. The paint and paste team were making progress on the walls upstairs.

Several of the team members cleaned up all the construction debris outside and tried to make the site safer for the workers. The Chilean concrete crew came and finished squaring up the window openings and removed the forms. The baño finally came–much to everyone's relief. I took some time to layout the lettering for the big sign for the church building and for a sign for along the road

Marilyn Jacobson was quite the artist, so she and some of Julae's friends primed the plywood and began painting the lettering. A few motorists and some of the neighbors stopped by to see what was going on and to ask what the building was going to be. I knew it was important for the sign to be put up.

We had settled into a routine, and a lot was getting done. With a team as large as we had, it required a lot of organization to keep everyone busy. A few of the team began to experience traveler's diarrhea, but most stayed healthy. Several team members got to go with Chuck to get supplies each day. The Construmart was quite similar to the large chain hardware and lumber stores in the USA. The women buying the groceries said the supermarkets were even bigger than those they frequented back home and added that the local supermarkets featured great fruits and vegetables that Chile is noted for

The tile work dragged on for days because of the sheer volume needed to be set, but progress was noticeable each day. More and more congregation members came to help, and it seemed our presence there was a great encouragement to them. They had met in rented facilities for some time and were eager to have their own building.

Saturday came, and we got to take a day off and go on a tour. One of the congregation members lived on a kiwi farm. We rode in Raoul's bus for forty miles or so out in the country to see it. We hiked around the farm and saw a real variety of plants. Hybrid kiwis were the main crop harvested, but they also raised figs, grapes, lemons, walnuts, and several varieties of hot peppers, paprika, and other crops. "Trellises supported the rows of kiwi plants about seven feet overhead and the kiwis were drip irrigated.

The team spent the afternoon eating nuts, sampling homemade wine, and visiting. What an interesting and relaxing day off we had! We  also visited the beach where I got to try some fishing. I casted out a hula popper lure into the surf. Fishing was a challenge, as I had to wait for the waves to recede and then run down to the waterline and quickly cast and run back up to escape the waves and to stay dry. I caught nothing but saw one big fish jump out of the water as he tried to get my lure

Later, out on a big wide pier that housed a restaurant and a number of shops, we got to sample lollapaloozas. It's a great treat of pineapple chunks, scoops of three kinds of ice cream, and whipped cream topped with a cherry in a hollowed-out pineapple rind. It's a meal! We did a little souvenir shopping at venders along the pier and around the beach. I found a sword made from a swordfish snout and some lapis lazuli jewelry that I got for my grandkids as well as some other trinkets. It was a great outing.

On Sunday morning, we planned to go to church with the congregation members. A local hotel had rented them a big room where they met for services each Sunday. The service was great. All the church members came and gave us greetings, hugs, handshakes, and air kisses. Nate Rieke really got into the Chilean greeting of an air kiss on the cheek with a big hug and went through the line more than once to re-greet the Chilean gals. We sang choruses that were familiar to us but were in Spanish. After the service, we got to go out to a military base north of the city where the congregation threw a big picnic for us. One would not find that kind of cooperation between government and the church in the USA. The centerpiece of the main table was intertwined Chilean and American flags. I wiped a tear from my eye at the sight

It was a fun afternoon with singing, dancing, and eating. The Chilean people we met were the most gracious and friendly folks I had ever met, and they did love a good party. It was great getting to know the congregation members better and to fellowship with them.

On Monday, it was back to work. When we arrived on the site and got ready for devotions, we discovered that no one had been assigned the duty, so I volunteered. I read one of my short canoe trip stories from my book. It is called "Minor Miracles," a story that explores the little things that happen to us in life that we often attribute to good luck or coincidence. I explained that if we take the time to really think about them, it is more often than not God's providence. I then tried to read an email I had gotten from my son, Matt, who was back home. Part of it was funny. He told me about his antics rounding up my wayward Labradors and the ticket he had gotten because of my dogs being at large. I had left on the trip with him promising to keep an eye on them, as he lived in a house only a block away from mine.

Then I said, "But now comes the best part. Matt hadn't gone to church for some time, and I had been praying for him to start." I broke down and couldn't finish reading the email to the group because it stated he, his wife, and his three kids all went to church together. Matt talked a bit about the sermon and that he would continue to go. It was a long-awaited answer to prayer, and Ross had to finish reading it for me. I was overcome by emotion so strong that it took some time to compose myself. I think everyone was touched and encouraged that

continued prayer for God's will to be done would bring good answers.

Marilyn and the girls had finished the second coat of paint on the big church sign, and preparations were made to hang the three 8-foot-long panels. It was like magic. When the signs went up, lots of people stopped to ask about the church. I think it was great advertising. The tile work continued for several more days. Ross and the others began assembling readymade kitchen cabinets that had arrived

The paste crew moved out to the handicap ramp. During the week, additional lumber came to build the raised stage at the front of the main room for the pastor. The ceiling grid was all hung after going through a number of concrete bits for the eye screws. Kimm's inventiveness helped, as he rigged the drill to  a lever hooked to the homemade stepladder so he could apply more force to drill into the stubborn concrete. Harvey got the power on and the

 lights working.

As the workweek neared its end, I remembered my promise to make a small stool for Isadora. We had lots of eucalyptus scraps left, so Kimm and I stayed late to see what we could make. Rather than a stool, I opted to make her a small rocking chair. In less than an hour, we had all the pieces cut out, sanded, and assembled. Three-year-old Isadora came along when Nadia and German arrived later to pick us up. Being so young, she

didn't understand it was for her, but she tried it out. We had cut out a small heart in the cross piece of the back. Nadia was in tears because she was so happy. They had tried for fourteen years to have a baby and had nearly given up hope, but then  along came Isadora. She was the most adorable child, with her long dark, curly hair, and she got a lot of attention. It made my day to see her ear-to-ear smile.

That night, we took our host families out for a steak dinner at a nice restaurant. It was the least we could do for them for putting us up for two weeks. We had an enjoyable evening, capped off by a stroll along the ocean. Isadora kept shouting, "Agua!" as the big waves rolled in. During our evening oceanside stroll we had to make an emergency stop for Harvey, as Montezuma's revenge struck, but he made it to a bathroom in time. Nearly all of us had a bit of that problem for a day or two during our stay, but for the most part, all of us stayed healthy, and no one got hurt.

On the evening of the last work day, pastor German invited all the members of the congregation to the first service in the new church. It was a great night. Our team leader presented awards to the team members. Many in the congregation gave small gifts to each of the team members. We had a joyous service, with singing and treats afterward. Kay Anne Rieke presented the church with a beautiful cross embroidered into a large white cloth that could serve as a banner. The celebration included communion and a short-translated sermon. The evening ended with a table full of snacks, pastries, and beverages. The congregation would not officially be meeting in the church for another couple of months, at least until the windows and doors could be installed. It was good for the congregation members who had not yet seen all that we accomplished to come and be encouraged.

As the week drew to a close, we had another day to go touring before we would leave, so we planned a picnic with our tour bus driver. We stopped at the historic house of a famous Chilean poet and took a tour. We rode a tour boat around the harbor and saw the big container ships and the Chilean navy. We had to keep reminding ourselves that Chile had been a country a couple hundred years longer than America

In the harbor, we saw giant brown pelicans with ten-foot wingspans. On the old docks and buoys, there were one-thousand-pound sea lions sunning themselves; they reek! Their smell was unlike anything I had ever smelled. It was overpowering and almost nauseating. We strolled on the beach for a time, and then we loaded up to take a short trip north to a small town famous for its llama and alpaca wool products.

I used to get a lot of kidding about all the souvenirs I took home, and that shopping day was no exception. I did get a bit carried away on this trip and had to put some of my souvenirs in others' suitcases for the trip home. My luggage would have been way overweight if it had been possible to stuff it all in my duffel bags. The llama blanket I bought must have weighed twenty pounds. It was as thick as a throw rug and very warm. I loved to souvenir shop and have quite a collection of items from all the trips I have taken

Our trek back to Reñaca took us along the coast highway for a couple of hours where we saw many interesting, expensive mansions and a most beautiful sunset over the ocean. It was a day to remember and one I recorded with dozens of photographs.

The last church service included long, tearful goodbyes to the group of Chilean Christians, who we now counted as our friends. I knew the goodbyes would be hard, but it caught some of the first-timers by surprise. It was really emotional. We exchanged email addresses and expressed our desire to return. We offered anyone who came to the USA a place to stay

After the service, it was time to head back to Santiago and the airport. A number of the congregation drove the fifty miles behind the tour bus just so they could say their final goodbyes. It was tears all over again at the airport. We exchanged kisses and hugs and waved our final goodbye as we went through the gate. Most of the team wished they could have stayed longer, and all wanted to return. It was a great trip. We left feeling that the church would grow exponentially in the large metro area. On our way home, we began talking about a return trip for the following spring. We all felt energized by our experience and prayed that God would bless our efforts to help this church get started.

Reñaca, Chile

February 2006

I mentioned to my friend Jesse Krech that a second trip was being planned to Reñaca, Chile, to continue the work of building the new church there. Jesse had been on the first trip there just a year earlier and had a vested interest in seeing the work continue. He agreed to go, and soon we were involved in planning meetings held in Clarkfield, Minnesota. Many of the team members being assembled had been on the first trip to Reñaca. We made plans with much prayer and we sent letters out seeking support for the trip by going or praying or giving. This group would be smaller than the first large group that traveled to help build the church.

We worked closely with the Ostleys, the missionaries in Reñaca, to find out what projects we would work on so that we would know what tools and materials to bring with us. Chuck mentioned that the church had the third story added on to the top of the building now and the building was all stucco coated and painted. The third story would have Sunday school rooms and an apartment for a live-in caretaker. He sent pictures. We were a bit upset when we noticed the big sign we had painted last time was no longer on the front of the church. Chuck said they had to take it down to stucco and paint and that now they wanted a more professional looking metal sign made and attached. Also, we would be working on getting the third-floor apartment ready for occupancy along with a number of things from our list from last time that still needed to be done. We found out that the law in Chile required public buildings to have a live-in caretaker, so part of the third floor of the church would be built into an apartment to house the person with that responsibility.

This time, the packing would involve a few different tools required to cut metal and drill holes in the concrete for the sign work. I decided to take a router and a sabre saw with a bunch of extra blades as well as the usual things that we would need. My battery powered tools would again make the trip, as some carpentry work would also need to be done. After several meetings and about three months of planning, the day came to assemble at my house for the usual last meal and the ride to the airport. We arranged extra drivers to return the cars to my house for free parking for the two weeks we would be gone. We ate at a restaurant serving buffet style again and soon were at the airport checking through security, which continued to get tighter all the time. We hiked to our departure gate and awaited our flight to Atlanta, where we would board the overnight flight to Santiago. All flights were on time, which was good because we had a short wait in Atlanta before we would board the big jet for the nine-hour night flight south to Santiago.

After so many mission trips, passing through the airports, finding gates, and going through customs, became quite routine. We had an easy and uneventful flight that night, but we all wished that the seats would have reclined more so we could have gotten more sound sleep. They packed a lot of people in a very small space. It would have been nice if we could have afforded first class rather than coach.

Shortly after sunrise, we arrived at the beautiful Santiago airport. I ran into a problem in customs when my luggage passed through. The officials made me open the bag with all my woodworking tools. I had packed hurriedly and had not cleaned the sawdust off my tools, so they would not release my luggage until we figured out a way to clean it up. They treated it like it was radioactive or something. Chuck rounded up a vacuum cleaner and a helper from Hertz, and we cleaned up all the sawdust. Then they made the young man helping us remove the bag from the vacuum and double bag it in plastic. We wasted about an hour and a half, and I have never heard the end of it. The customs officials also pulled the two feathers out of my leather hat, saying, "No plumba." I guess the avian flu going around had everyone being extra cautious.

At the time, Santiago had about five million people and was a thriving metropolis. They even had subways there. We loaded our heavy luggage aboard Raoul's tour bus for the hour-and-a-half ride to the coast

where Reñaca is located. Because Santiago is inland about fifty or sixty miles from the ocean, we'd have to take the bus on the last leg of the trip. We looked forward to arriving at the church and seeing old friends again. Upon arrival, we were surprised at how different the church looked, with its coat of coral red stucco and the third story above. The arches gave it a definite Spanish flair.

We took a quick tour of the building and noted that all the doors and windows were now in and that the concrete workers were starting to build the main entryway that would house the stairway to the second floor. For now, our access was by ladder. All the building materials would have to be roped up to the third floor. The lack of a stairway promised to make work slow and difficult.

The host families arrived to take us to the homes where we would stay for the two weeks. Harvey and I would bunk at Pastor German's new rental house, which was quite a bit nicer than his old one. It was close enough to the church that we could walk to work and not have to climb the giant hill behind the church.

Our first work day began with devotions that we all would take turns giving. We then discussed the projects set before us and divided up the team to begin the work. There was wall sheetrock to hoist up to the third floor as well as studs to divide the large third floor room into Sunday school rooms. We needed to build the room divisions on top of the big three-foot-high concrete beams that held the ceiling of the floor below. Two of them spanned the entire depth of the room. They had mistakenly been built on top of the floor rather than under it. The sewer pipes again had not been set in the concrete floor of the apartment bathroom, so we had to put them together and pour a new floor on top of the already existing one, which made for one step up to get into the bathroom as well as the kitchen.

Nate and Jesse began framing the walls, and I began measuring and cutting stair jacks to build a short flight of stairs up, over, and down the two big beams. That was the only way to get between the Sunday school rooms. After the wall studs were nailed together, the sheetrock team came and put up the pink-colored sheetrock. Then the mudders followed, covering the nail heads and taping the seams to make a smooth wall ready for the painters who followed soon after. The walls were all done within about four days. Completing the steps made getting between the rooms much easier.

Lots of little jobs were left to do from the last teams trip. Team members tackled putting up towel bars and toilet paper holders. Some additional kitchen cabinets were installed by a couple of the guys, along with locks and handles for the doors. Some of the gals potted plants and planted a flowerbed to beautify the front of the church. One of the team members built two large masonry flower and shrub boxes above the second-floor entryway, which would someday be filled with dirt and large plants over the doorway and level with the third floor.

Chuck searched for and finally found a one-meter-by-three-meter-piece of sheet aluminum with which we were to make the new sign. We began designing the lettering to say, "Alianza ye Missionera Christiana," along with the logo of the CMA church, which is used world-wide.

We drew the letters on heavy cardboard, cut them out, and tacked them to a long stick in a line. Then two team members on ladders held them up against the building where we thought they should go. We walked back to the street to see where the sign would look the best. The sheet of aluminum cost a couple hundred dollars, and we didn't want to make any mistakes. The sign looked good, and after much discussion, we decided where to position it. We bought a length of copper pipe, which we cut up into dozens of two-inch lengths for stand-off bushings so the shadow of the sign would emphasize the letters as it fell on the building. We rounded up a black magic marker and traced all the letters onto the aluminum sheet. By positioning them carefully, we found they all just fit.

The next day was the day to tour the harbor and the city. I had seen all those sights the last trip, so I volunteered to stay behind and work at the church alone. I wanted to try to cut out all the lettering so the next work day we could begin to put up the sign. I wished all rest of the team a fun time. The next morning, I made my way to the church and let myself in with the keys I had borrowed from Pastor German

It was a pleasantly cool day, so I set up sawhorses in the parking lot right in front of the church and ran a power cord out to begin work. The aluminum sheet with the letters traced on it was about three-sixteenths of an inch thick. First, I tried my router with a narrow bit. It got about three inches and then filled up the blade with melted aluminum. Not good! Then I put a metal cutting blade in the sabre saw, and it cut better, but as the blade heated up, the same thing happened. All the teeth plugged up with melted aluminum. I began to worry that we would have to pay a lot for a machinist to do the cutting. Just to see what would happen I put a coarse tooth wood cutting blade in the sabre saw, and it worked beautifully. There were a lot of letters to cut out, so I began the long task.

By lunchtime, I had a third of the letters cut out. I took a break and made myself a couple of sandwiches and then went back to work. A big yellow Labrador dog wandered up to me and sat and watched me work. Then he scratched himself a hole in the sand and lay down in it and took a nap all afternoon while I continued to cut. I went through six sawblades and had to pause at times to let the saw cool down, but by the end of the afternoon, all the letters were cut out. I dug out my random orbit sander and polished the metal. Then I marked with a dot all the points where the letters would have to be fastened to the wall. I figured we would need to drill about one hundred holes in the concrete to get everything mounted.

The next work day, we drilled between two and four holes in each letter and cut in a countersink so the bolts we had chosen would lay flat with the surface of the letters. Jesse and Nate set up scaffolding and began the arduous task of drilling all those holes. We tapped a threaded anchor into each hole when it was finished and mounted the letters. Slowly they began to form the words. The letters stood out about two inches from the stucco and looked professional. We used and broke dozens of masonry drill bits. Often, Jesse and Nate would run into reinforcing rod in the concrete when they tried to drill a hole. As work on the sign progressed, pedestrians stopped out on the sidewalk

occasionally to see what the sign would say. Some stopped to chat. The sign was finished in time for Sunday services the next day. A young college-age girl came to services that Sunday morning. The sign was a pleasant surprise she said because back home in the USA, the CMA is the church she attended. She was in Chile doing work with the Wycliffe Bible translators. She continued to attend until her stay in Chile was over.

Sunday was a fun day where we got to meet with many of the congregation members who we remembered from the last trip down. They loved having a place to meet up on the second floor, and the service was joyous. I volunteered to give my testimony. Sheryl translated as I stated that I always felt I was a Christian and grew up in a Christian home but had lacked spark. I talked about the old Volkswagen Beetle car that sat abandoned in the lot next to the church. I said it was a car and one could put gas in the tank, but if the battery had no spark, it could never start and would never get anyone anywhere. I explained that I was like that car. I looked like a Christian, and I knew a lot about the Bible, but without that charge–that poke from the Holy Spirit–I was no good to the Lord and would never lead anyone to Him. Until someone led me to a true understanding of what Christ did for me, I lacked that spark. The congregation chuckled at my analogy and nodded their understanding.

In the afternoon, we spent time with our host families. German took us for a walk along the sea wall, where we could see crabs and starfish down in the ocean tidal pools along with dozens of sea urchins. As we spent time in Reñaca, we were able to see what a beautiful city it was, with nicely trimmed trees and bushes and attractive and historic buildings. Chuck told us it was like Beverly Hills back home, a wealthy suburb. In Chile, in 2006, about eighty-five percent of the population was Catholic. The average Chilean had the opinion that if one is wealthy, he or she is Catholic and if poor, Protestant. Thus, there was a difficulty in starting a Protestant church in a wealthy neighborhood, but if doing so, there was a need to have the church structure look attractive and well built.

After our pleasant afternoon with our host families we returned to their home. That night we played more Scrabble, and I dug out my acrylic paints and painted a couple small pictures of what the Boundary Waters looked like in northern Minnesota. German and Nadia liked the small paintings.

Back at work the next morning, we began painting the upstairs Sunday school rooms and the apartment the caretaker would live in. Our to-do list was getting smaller. Harvey worked ahead of the sheet-rockers to get outlets and switches installed and to get the fluorescent lights hung. The small parking lot looked nice as the women finished their work with the large potted plants. Several team members painted the handicap ramp to the second floor as well as the rest of the stucco below it. Julae, the Ostley's daughter, and some of her friends skipped classes and helped with tiling the two wide steps, which led into the lower level of the church. They also took on the project of painting a couple of signs for along the road to attract people to the church. More and more, the building took on a finished look.

Chuck hired more competent concrete contractors and they tore down some of the stairway wall that had been built crooked by the original builders. They began forming the stairway and the underlying walls that would become the main entry to the church. The stairway would give us easy access to the third floor and provide the walls for two rooms below for the men's and women's bathrooms. The next team would tile these rooms and install the plumbing. (unknown to me, I would be leading that group in less than a year). We also built the raised stage in the front of the church, which would later be carpeted by the Chileans. Harvey installed the conduit for all the wiring for electricity and microphone wires.

On the second Sunday, we departed after church with a number of the congregation members following us for a short trip north up the coast. Nate Rieke wanted to be baptized in the Pacific Ocean! When we arrived at the spot, we gathered on the beach. The air was pretty warm, but it was quite breezy, and big rollers were coming in. Pastor German and Ross, Nate's dad, accompanied him out to about waist deep water and carefully timed the phrase, "Baptize you in the name of the Father, Son, and Holy Ghost," to the incoming rollers and dunked him perfectly as a big roller came in and almost knocked them all off their feet. It was great fun and a good witness to the congregation of Nate's faith. Afterward, just up the road, we stopped at a restaurant where we all ate a wonderful dinner and treated our hosts. I had a meal of tasty queenfish, which is pretty popular in Chile.

Alas, the time to depart was upon us, so we all gathered at the church for a going away party. We exchanged gifts, and shed tears. We said good bye to all the friends we had made. After the party, when all our new Chilean friends had left for home, we packed up our tools and readied our luggage for the trip. In the morning, we would ride the bus back to Santiago for our flight back home. The bus trip back was routine, and we had a little time to shop in Santiago before boarding our plane. I felt so moved by the trips I had taken that I promised myself if it were possible, I would like to take Matt and or the grandkids, Zack and Becca, on the next trip. My prayers were answered less than a year later, as I was able to take the grandkids on the first of two mission trips they would take to Chile.

Reñaca, Chile

---⊗⊗⊗---

July 2006

I volunteered to take another trip to Reñaca, Chile. The return trip was
in the planning stages and on the heels of the last one to that church.
For the first time, The Clarkfield church named me as the leader of
the group. The team had many of the usual members from Clarkfield.
Gordy Geisfeld from Echo was along for his second or third trip, but
it was a first trip for his wife. Tim from Hibbing, Minnesota, was a
newcomer as was Clair from Vesta, Minnesota. Brenda and her son,
Jake, from Kandiyohi, were not only newcomers, but they had never
been out of the country or even out of Minnesota and had never been
on a Jet. It was going to be especially interesting, as I was taking Zack
and Rebeccah, my grandchildren, along as well for their first trip. We
figured the kids would connect with each other pretty well, and as it
worked out, they did.

This was my last trip to Reñaca, but the Clarkfield church sent one
more team about a year later. By this time, the church was well on the
way to completion of three of four stages of construction. Our projects
this time were going to be to try to waterproof parts of the upstairs and
reroute drainage water coming down the hill. We had toilets, sinks, and
countertops to install in both bathrooms; there was also a lot of ceramic
tile work we could tackle in the bathrooms. We had landscaping to do
and new kitchen cabinets to install. Also, we could do more painting and
wall pasting in the upstairs apartment. In Chile, all public buildings had

ROY CERNY

to have a live-in caretaker, so the church had to create a small apartment for this person to use.

The team members arrived at my house. Among them were three children aged ten to twelve, who were all pretty excited. It was like dribbling three basketballs at once. My son, Matt; his wife, Michelle; and my friend Mark McCoy served as drivers to return the vehicles to my house for the two weeks we would be gone. We had our usual going away meal and headed to the airport. All went well until our departure became delayed. The longer we waited, the more worried I became that we would miss our connecting flight in Atlanta

I finally went up to the ticket counter and asked, "Why are we delayed?" I found out that our plane was waiting to pick up a spare tire before it could go to Atlanta and the tire had not yet arrived. I asked the attendant to ask our overnight connecting flight to Chile to wait for us, as it was critical we get on board or we would lose time for our mission work. He said he would see what he could do

We finally took off two hours late. It was doubtful we would get to our connecting flight. We arrived in Atlanta a couple hours later and rushed to our gate because our Chile flight was still there. We were denied boarding, though. They had given our seats to others. I was so disheartened. They gave us vouchers for food and rooms at a local semi-seedy motel, but that didn't make up the time lost. Our flight went to Chile only once a day, so we couldn't leave till the next evening. We were disappointed but determined to make the best of it.

We went out to eat a late supper and decided that in the morning we would get together for breakfast to see if we could rent a tour bus for a day and see some of the sights of Atlanta, sights such as the underground mall and the Coke Museum. At least this gave us some interesting things to do until our flight left the next evening. We rented a bus, and by splitting the costs and using some of our slush fund money, it was not too expensive. We had an interesting day, ate supper on the airline's dime, and met again at the airport. This time we were able to board even though we got the worst seats available. We left on time, and between movies, a couple of paperbacks, and dozing on and off, we finally landed in Santiago. Then we worked our way through customs. Raoul again arrived with his tour bus, and we boarded with our luggage for the trip to the church.

Upon our arrival, we discovered that the Chilean contractors had constructed a new entryway and landing, with two rooms beneath the landing for the bathrooms, but the forms for the poured entryway floor had to stay in place for several days before the bracing could be taken down. The entryway floor was the ceiling to the two bathrooms below, so our work on the bathrooms was on hold for a time.

Our host families came and took us to their homes. Zack, Becca, and I stayed with the Ostleys. Becca moved into Julae's room and was treated like a little sister. They became tighter than glue. Zack and I bunked together. The Ostley's had been missionaries to Chile for many years and were originally from the Clarkfield church.

In the morning, our hosts drove us to the church, where we had our devotions and then broke into teams. I appointed Becca the task of

assistant cook, and Zack became the team's tool quartermaster. The Architects planned for the Reñaca church to be made mostly of poured concrete and dug into a steep hill. The contractors had built it three stories high, and each floor projected like stacked blocks a little deeper into the hillside. Zack and Tim began excavating a ditch above the third story of the church to intercept the runoff from the hill and channel it around the outside of the building so it wouldn't run onto the roof, which was level with the hillside. That seemed to help a great deal with the leakage problems they were having.

Chuck had purchased some prefabricated cabinets, and they had to be put up in the kitchen. Lois, one of our team members on her first mission trip, graciously offered to buy a large set of silverware for the church kitchen.

Several team members worked on setting tile on the outside stairs and a ramp into the lower level of

the church. They also formed and poured some concrete to complete the ramp and step area.

Before supper, we had a ring exchange ceremony for Kimm and Sheryl, as they were planning a wedding soon. Kimm had first met Sheryl on the mission trip to Antofagasta, where she had been working with the pastor there to start an Alliance Church. In Chile, the ceremony was important, and the church then would put its stamp of approval on the engagement. It was half in fun and half serious. It was like a roast with singing and scriptures thrown in.

After our work day, Chuck and Betty Ostley had a marriage encounter planning meeting at the church, so the kids and I hiked the four blocks uphill to their house. Tough exercise for the legs! When Chuck and Betty arrived, we gave them gifts of food that we had packed for them from home. These included Wheat Chex^{tm} for Chuck, because it's his favorite cereal and not available in Chile, and gourmet tea and coffee for Betty to try. We also presented the whole family with a game of Scrabble and played our first game later that night. Becca won, and I ended up with the lowest score for the four of us who played.

Kimm's devotions in the morning explained that the Lord doesn't keep us from adversity and trials but does give us the strength to withstand them. That was good advice for directing our prayers. So far everyone's health was holding up and there were no cases of traveler's diarrhea. We were not quite caught up on the sleep we had missed from the airplane trip, though. At least the time change was only one hour. Betty said she would try to take the kids horseback riding on the beach on our upcoming day off. Becca was ecstatic!

The work on this day was nasty. The kids got to brush a black tar waterproofing substance on the walls up on the third floor. The contractor had done the concrete work poorly, and they had applied no waterproofing to the outside walls before they were backfilled, so it had to be put on the inside of the walls. What a messy job! Work continued on the tile and soon the bracing would come out of the bathroom area so we could get to work in there.

That evening, there was a Christian concert, and all the teenagers wanted to go. Hector, a congregation member from church, offered to take them, but he spoke no English, so the kids were a bit reluctant to go. Tim from our team agreed to go along as a chaperone, and then the teens were more eager. I knew they would have a good time.

It was winter in Chile, but it was not very cold. We wore sweatshirts in the morning and tee shirts by afternoon. The fog and heavy dew usually burned off by noon. Oranges and Lemons were at their peak of flavor, and there were many groves out in the countryside around town. Some trees had shed their leaves while others had not, strange seasons. We saw giant slugs crawling around on damp mornings. I had heard they do a lot of damage to flowers and vegetables.

In the city at night, there was a constant barrage of background noise consisting of dogs barking. Most homes had pets, but there was also a large population of strays. Typical homes in Chile were small and were on tiny lots. That saved a lot of money for the city because it meant fewer roads, sewer pipes, power lines, and streetlights. People went to parks for recreation, the ocean to kayak or sunbathe, or to the Andes Mountains to go skiing. All were close by

The average Chilean had enough disposable income to invest in sports or recreation and have hobbies. From the experiences I had there, I would say most Chileans live a much healthier life style than most Americans. The majorities of the homes we saw in Reñaca were concrete and had a lot of ceramic tile work in them. Many had multiple bathrooms. Most had on-demand hot water heaters, which were tricky to get to work right. The temperature of the water was warmer the slower we ran it because it had more time to heat up as it passed through the heater.

On Saturday, the kids went horseback riding. Becca had to switch horses, as her first horse wouldn't go. The next one was much faster, causing Becca's shoe to slip off, but she hung on as it galloped across the sandy beach. They had a lot of fun. Kimm, Harvey, and Sheryl took a couple days off to travel to her old church in the north of Chile to visit friends.

The Chilean contractors removed the support posts on that Monday, so the tilework could finally begin in the bathrooms. Gordy already had preassembled all the toilets and mounted all the sink faucets. We varnished the tops of the tables, but the varnish wasn't compatible with the surface, and it began to peel right away. We began to put rubber edging on the twenty tables we had built last time, but it was a slow process. We corrected the out of plumb entry doors, and then removed some tiles and remounted them in a raised row to form a threshold to stop water from seeping under the doors. Harvey laid in the new wiring for the bathrooms. We began work on the laminate countertops and found

that the bathroom wall had about a two-inch hump in it. The counter had to be cut and re-joined in the middle to follow the hump in the wall.

After devotions ended each morning, we sang hymns along with Betty's flute and Tim's guitar. With their sweet accompaniment, the songs were several steps up from making a joyful noise to the Lord. As each workday passed, we got more done, but our time in Chile was beginning to run out.

Saturday evening for supper we had chili because it was a chilly day in Chile; sorry, I just couldn't help myself. The next day we planned to have Sunday services and meet the rest of the congregation members. Sunday afternoon, Betty and Julae took the bus to Santiago about fifty miles away so Julae could say goodbye to one of her friends going off to college. Chuck took Zack, Becca, and me shopping downtown, where we found some nice alpaca jackets in colors the kids liked for about twenty dollars each.

The work on Monday was to begin with the ceramic tile in the two bathrooms, the damas (women's) and the varóns (men's). The tile work went quite slowly because of the unevenness of the walls and the difficulty to get the tile to lay flat. As progress was made, we

kept finding more projects to do. Tim painted the unfinished part of the exterior stucco a nice coral red color. The two-story side of the church was tricky to do because he had to stand on a very narrow ledge.

Becca spent the night at Pastor German and Nadia's house, because their two teenage nieces were there, and they had struck up quite a friendship trying to teach each other Spanish and English. Becca had a year of Spanish in school and got to practice using it.

Zack and I spent the night watching TV in Spanish at the Ostleys. Their house was nice, with laminated wood floors, three baths, and on-demand hot water. They had a small, fenced concrete patio for a front yard but no back yard at all. My grandkids seemed to be having a lot of fun and learning a lot about Chilean culture. Becca loved the Ostley's cat named Sunshine.

Church services on the second Sunday lasted two and a half hours and were held in the upstairs sanctuary. Chuck translated the Spanish sermon. We heard familiar hymns in Spanish. We shook hands with all the men and hugged all the women, as is the custom there. There were about one hundred and twenty-five in attendance, and we got to meet many old friends we had made from our previous two trips there. The grand kids seemed to make friends easily. It was fun watching them trying to communicate with everyone. I swear Zack grew an inch that week. His dress pants didn't fit, so we had to make a quick trip downtown to get him a new pair with a waist of ninety centimeters so he would have something to wear for church. Afterward, we went to eat at Reggie's, a local restaurant, for a nice meal of steak and papas (potatoes).

On Monday, beginning our second full week of work, we made up a to-do list after our morning devotions. The list had many more things on it than we could possibly finish, so we tried to do the most important items first. Most of the team had blended in well with the local cultures, but there had been a few hiccups. The kids wanted to have fun, and sometimes it was a bit difficult to keep them on task, but as a whole, I was very proud of them. We learned more and more Spanish words and went home exhausted each night. All the healthy food and especially all the coffee and tea were fouling up my body chemistry and caused me to have to get up to go to the bathroom way more often than usual.

Our full team got back to work. Zack had an especially tough day, as his assignment was to pick-ax the ditch on the hill above the church to divert the water coming down the hill. Plans were to install a concrete culvert to make it a permanent fix. The contractors concrete work was done poorly, and plans were not closely followed, so many problems developed since the installation. The contractors neglected to do waterproofing to the outside, and they had installed the concrete beams for the second-floor ceiling above the floor instead of below it. Their error caused the room layout on the third floor many problems, as we had to build steps over the three-foot-high beams.

Back at work, we were starting to run into a time crunch. We had only two and a half days left, and we were all crowded into the bathrooms, trying to get them tiled and the sinks and toilets installed. Earlier in the week we also experienced our first temblor(earthquake). I was sitting at the computer and it rocked a bit followed by a long rumble that echoed down the oceanfront like a distant peal of thunder. Nobody got too excited as they are common in Chile. We had a bit of a setback from a violent thunderstorm the night before. Water from all the rain ran into the lower level of the church and got a lot of the boxes of tile wet and ruined some of the bags of grout that Chuck had purchased. The tile and grouting were the most important projects left to do. We were trying hard to get the bathrooms functional but weren't able to get as far as we wanted. Our to-do list had been whittled down a bit, but there were lots of items still on it that would have to wait for the next team to arrive.

As our time in Chile ended, Chuck said the airline may cut our luggage weight limit because we have all gained a few pounds while there. Tim was still busy downloading pictures everyone had taken onto the computer. Chuck said Julae got her report card and got all A grades. He thanked me for helping her with her chemistry homework. That night the grandkids went with Julae to her school program. It was a concert with a "Back-to-the-'50s" theme. Zack said it was "Beatlemania." Becca commented on how the boys all looked at her and Julae with their long blonde hair. They had a blast.

On our last day off, we all piled into the bus and got a driving tour of the city. We were able to go to the top of the bluff over the city, where we could see the whole harbor. The Chilean navy ships were anchored a mile or so out from shore. Close by them was a large floating dry dock that was interesting. It consisted of two giant, long steel boxes that were floating side by side, about one hundred feet apart. The boxes were each approximately one thousand feet long and maybe one hundred and fifty feet tall and about seventy-five feet wide. A steel floor between but beneath the boxes held them in place. If a ship needed to be worked on, the boxes were pumped full of water until they sank deep enough for the ship to maneuver itself in between the boxes. The water was pumped back out and the boxes floated up, lifting a ship, weighing thousands of tons, right out of the water so the hull could be worked on. After the repairs were made or the barnacles cleaned off, the process was reversed and the ship was floated back out. Several large freighters had their huge cargo of containers unloaded by the giant cranes. The cranes were over three hundred feet tall and wide and long enough to span an entire container ship. The two enormous cranes were assembled by ironworkers and shipped on a giant barge all the way from Holland

The harbor had lots of small fishing boats at anchor because of the swells from the big storm the night before. Later, we rode around the harbor on a launch to see the city from the ocean view. We saw dozens of smelly sea lions on the harbor buoys and got closer looks at the small fishing boats. The weather was sunny, and it was a great outing for the team.

We ate out at a small seafood restaurant, and for dessert, I treated the grandkids to a lollapalooza. To make one the venders hollowed out pineapples and filled the rinds back up with chopped pineapple, three kinds of ice cream, chocolate syrup, and whipped cream. Then they were topped with a vanilla wafer and a cherry. The kids were so full they could hardly walk. We also rode up to the top of the bluff on a tram pulled up the steep hill by a cable. Much of the city's residential areas were perched precariously up the steep hillsides. Eight years later, much of the area we saw would be burned up by a catastrophic fire in the city of Valparaíso, which destroyed about two thousand homes and killed a number of people.

This was our last day to work on the church. It was a beautiful building, having many arches and all the stucco painted a striking coral red color. The cut-out aluminum sign, "Alianza Christiana y Missionera" (Alliance of Christians and Missionaries), and the accompanying logo of the church that we made and installed on the previous trip looked very professional. In the USA the church is called the Christian and Missionary Alliance or CMA.The next team would have to finish the work on the church. I would not be able to go, as it was coming too close on the heels of this trip, and I had gone to Chile twice in the span of a year and needed to take a break. As the church grows in size, there was a plan for building a main sanctuary that would seat six hundred people but that project would be several years or more away.

On the last day, we packed up our tools and said goodbye to the congregation members helping us that day. Back at the Ostley's, we had sharing time. We gave Julae a new purse, and Betty got an Alpaca jacket. The kids got billfolds, and Becca got a lapis lazuli cross on a necklace. It was a semi-precious stone similar to turquois, which is found only in Chile and Afghanistan. We were all feeling sad that our time in Chile was nearly over.

In the morning, we all met at the church and loaded our luggage in the bus and then headed for the airport. The long flight home was a nonstop narrative from the grandkids about the great time they had. We had no problems with late flights or getting through customs. After arriving home, I got busy unpacking and washing clothes. It was back to reality. I was thinking about work for the next day. It was good to be home but difficult to come back down to earth after such a mountaintop experience.

Antofagasta, Chile

T his mission trip was born out of a need to expand the church in Antofagasta, as it had grown its congregation considerably since we were there a few years previously. It was going to be an exciting trip because I was taking Zack and Becca, my two grandchildren, along for their second mission trip experience. The team for this trip consisted of eight people. Kimm and Sheryl, who had recently married; Pat Dotey (Sheryl's aunt); Harvey; myself; the two grandkids, Zack and Becca; and my friend Mark McCoy. It was a small team, but we were eager to serve the Lord. We felt empowered and ready for this trip.

All team members except for Mark were mission trip veterans. I had mentioned to my friend Mark, who was a new Christian, that he should consider going on a mission trip with us. His first reaction was "No way. I can't afford it." He did think it would be fun and a good experience, though. I talked to him more about going and said, "If you have it in your heart to go and let the Lord lead, money will not be an issue." He was open to the idea to go, and soon, donations came in. Mark had a lot of friends in the alcohol and drug abuse recovery programs and several gave to help him be able to go. The Clarkfield church, as well, helped out with funds. In no time, Mark was the first one to have all his costs paid, and his anticipation for the trip began to build. I helped him plan what to take along and told him what to expect.

Soon, the departure day arrived, and we did the usual arrangement of having everyone meet at my house. We went out to eat at the nearby buffet-style restaurant for our last American meal for the next couple of weeks. Because the trip was in July, the forty pound luggage restrictions had been eased somewhat and now we each could take two suitcases of fifty pounds each. We checked our weights on the bathroom scale and did some last-minute shuffling to avoid overweight cases. Kimm distributed packages of special Torx screws that we found so helpful in building. We spread out about fifty pounds of them between team members whose suitcases could hold more weight.

After our meal, we drove to the Minneapolis-St Paul Airport and waited for our flight to Dallas. From there, we would board a large jet for the overnight flight to Santiago. On that flight, Mark spent a great deal of time standing because of pain in his leg. He was badly injured in a motorcycle accident a few years before and still suffered from its effects. Early in the morning, we landed in Chile and had to go through customs. Then we boarded a smaller Lan-Chile jet for the in-country flight back north, nearly one thousand miles to Antofagasta. Mark finally realized that the mission trip was actually going to happen when he stepped off the jet with the rest of the team.

The airport was a few miles north of the city of Antofagasta, a teaming metropolis of about three hundred thousand souls. The church had provided a bus to transport our team and the luggage into town where we would meet our host families. Zack and I got to stay with a family who lived in a three-bedroom apartment with their daughter. Becca stayed with an elderly woman close to the church, and Mark got to stay with Jorje, one of the church elders, who had a number of children.

Upon arrival at the church the next morning, we had our usual devotions and then got to meet with the Jefe (foreman) of the project. Sheryl interpreted, and he explained what we were to do to move the project forward. What had been done so far was the

removal of the steel roof. The first few days of our work were to be the demolition of the gable end walls so that all the walls would be the same height. Then we would excavate through the old concrete floor creating fifteen square holes about a meter on each side and a meter deep. The holes were for footings for columns that would support a poured concrete floor overhead, which would be the start for the second story of the church. The second story would be the new sanctuary, as the large first floor room had become just too small for the growing congregation.

The work was noisy, dusty, dirty, and a bit dangerous on the shaky homemade scaffolding. The foreman had two electric jackhammers for us to use, and even Becca tried running one for a while but kept getting

it stuck, as she didn't have the weight to move it around. Within two days, we had almost all the high parts of the walls demolished, which would have projected into the new floor had we not broken them down. The biggest difficulty was cutting all the rebar out of the crumbling concrete.

We used the battery-powered reciprocating saws we had taken along quite a bit. To that point in the trip, our team had suffered only a skinned shin, but one of the Chilean workers had cut his hand, and the Chilean

foreman fell in a footing hole and gashed his leg badly and needed to get stitches.

The next day, we went to Sunday school with the church members, then souvenir shopping, and ate downtown at a McDonalds (yes, even in Chile there are McDonalds). They also had KFC, TGI Fridays, Dominos, and Pizza Hut. We found that America is a big trading partner with Chile, and much of the fruit in our grocery stores in the U.S. comes from Chile. After a day out shopping, we headed back to the host homes and readied for the main church service, which they were holding that Sunday evening.

For better understanding of the area, I believe a description of the city of Antofagasta and what life there was like there might be enjoyable. The city was comparable to Duluth, Minnesota, as it is about twenty-five miles long and a mile wide. Instead of nestling up to Lake Superior like Duluth, Antofagasta hugs the Pacific Ocean and extends up into the hills above the city, which were devoid of any vegetation .

The roads were all pretty narrow, but that did not slow the drivers down at all. Most of the cars were tiny three or four cylinder vehicles, displacing one liter or less of engine size. Chile does not manufacture any cars, so all were imported, and many I had never heard of. We had seen Peugeots and Citroens from France, Laddas from Russia, and Kias, Hyundais, and Daihatsus from Korea. There were some American Chevy Sparks and Jeep Liberties as well as the Brazilian imported Chevy Luv. From China, we saw Zotyes, Changan Bennis, and Great Walls. We saw cars from India and a curious SUV called a Galloper. There were many others I cannot recall, but for a car buff, it was interesting. Many of the trucks were Volvos or Mercedes, and a big share of vehicles ran on diesel, as that afforded better mileage and was cheaper to operate and more efficient than gasoline. Gasoline had to be imported, as Chile had little and only a small amount of coal. Most of the cars seemed pretty new, which reflected on the health of the Chilean economy.

I learned that what Chile lacks in fossil fuels is more than made up for in its mineral wealth. Chile supplies about one third of the world's copper. It has vast supplies of Lithium, which is used to make batteries. It has lots of rare earth metals and also valuable metals like molybdenum and platinum. It has perhaps the largest supply of natural nitrate salts for fertilizer anywhere in the world in the Atacama Desert

Five trainloads of copper ingots went right past the church where we were working every day on their way to the storage area at the port. Chile could control the price of copper by how much they shipped out of the port. If prices were deemed too low they stopped shipping copper and switched to shipping molybdenum until the prices rose. The trains that hauled the copper from the mines ran on narrow gauge tracks and had small locomotives. They could pull only five flatcars of ingots at a time because copper is so heavy. Each flatbed carload was worth about 250 thousand dollars, so there was about a million and a quarter dollars-worth going by the church each time a train passed. Ten percent of the income for the government comes from the copper mines in the desert.

The Chilean people were very friendly and cordial. The gals greeted us with hugs and air kisses on our cheeks, and the guys greeted by shaking hands and patting us on our backs. The church services were similar to ours with many of the same hymns and choruses but sung in Spanish.

The Chilean food we ate was not very spicy, but they sure liked cilantro. Other specialties we encountered included Chilean-made wines and very good pastries. They also loved salads. Pan (bread) and papas (potatoes) were their chief sources of starch. They ate lots of fruits and vegetables and very little soda pop or junk food.

Drinks were usually instant coffee, brewed tea, or mixed up juices. Chileans were quite weight conscious and were careful not to overeat. They ate far healthier than Americans. Many of the women we met in Chile could have been models.

The weather in northern Chile was um…shall we say dry and clear. It is close enough to the equator that winter is mild on the coast as the temperature is controlled by the ocean to a great degree. Some mornings there was a bit of fog that rolled in off the ocean, sometimes a bit of dew. Often it was hazy. It was weird seeing all the bare soil on the hills above the city, but the weather there does not support much life. Any greenery we saw was because someone supplied water otherwise bare soil was everywhere. The last time it rained significantly there was in 1992. The inch of rain they got caused a massive mud slide in the middle of the night and killed two hundred and twenty people as they slept. Our host family emailed us before we came down on this trip all excited because they had gotten two millimeters of rain. That would not have been enough to wet the sidewalk.

We saw pigeons, sparrows, one hawk, and a few hummingbirds as well but little else for wildlife. No 'skeeters or flies either. Nearly every family had pets, and if they didn't have one, there were dozens of strays roaming the streets they could choose from. Chileans often painted their houses loud, garish colors, probably to counteract the depressive gray and browns of the landscape.

Back at work the next day, we found out we still had to jackhammer out five more footings, so the cement work was postponed a few more days. As we excavated the holes, we found big chunks of nitrate salt in with the soil. The nitrate salt would have made a good fertilizer if we had ground it up. For our work, however, its presence meant we had to line the holes we dug with plastic so that soil moisture did not cause the salt to eat the reinforcing rods that we put in the forms.

The gals enlisted Becca to help them teach English to some of the other ladies and the children. When she finished her classes, she

helped Harvey with running plastic conduit for the electrical wiring. She was also learning how to wire tie rebar together to make cages to put inside the concrete forms for extra strength. Zack and Becca were doing outstanding work, and I was so proud of how they were pitching in to help and how they interacted with the Chileans.

We were then pouring concrete into all the excavated and lined holes we had made for footings. Mark had become the head concrete

honcho, mixing all the concrete with a rented cement mixer. After he mixed the concrete, we wheelbarrowed it to the holes. We had trundled out at least two big dump-truck loads of debris, and we were replacing all that with concrete. Each footing had four steel reinforcing rods sticking up out of the floor to tie the footings to the pillars, which we still needed to form.

When we first started mixing the concrete, I was concerned that our foreman was skimping a bit on the Portland cement in the concrete mix. I knew the father at my host family was a safety inspector at the mines, so I set out to ask him what the ratio of sand to gravel to Portland should be when concrete was to be made. It took about an hour and a lot of looking up of Spanish words, but he finally understood what I wanted to know. He also became concerned and took the next day off from his work and came to the church to offer his knowledge about concrete. He had a discussion with the foreman and helped him understand what the ratio should be for the most strength.

The next step of construction was to wire each of the rebar cages to the four rods coming out of the floor at each column location. Then we built and placed a plywood box about sixteen inches square and eight feet tall around each rebar cage to make a reinforced column form that we then filled with concrete and vibrated to get all the air pockets out of it. The first one that we filled blew apart from the pressure, so we found we had to screw the forms together, rather than nailing them to make them  stronger.. It was backbreaking work passing buckets of concrete up to a person on scaffolding for them to then dump the concrete into the forms. It would take several days to get all the columns poured.

After we made progress on some of the work, we were able to take a mini vacation out into the desert. We rented a diesel pickup with a crew cab and borrowed the pickup from my host family's father and then set out to go into the Atacama desert. We stopped and got pictures at the big boulder along the road that marked the Tropic of Capricorn. The sign we had posted several years before pointing to Wall Drug in South Dakota was no longer there. We visited the abandoned nitrate mining towns and saw the graves of all the people who had died in the desert trying to get rich mining the nitrates. We continued on to the town of Calama, where the giant Chuquicamata copper mine is.

The mine is an open pit about two miles across and twenty-five hundred feet deep. The mine trucks we saw had sixteen-foot-tall tires and could haul five hundred tons at a time. They were seventy feet tall when the dump box was raised and cost several million dollars apiece. We were disappointed that we were too late in the day to take an official tour, so we continued on to the small town (five thousand) of San Pedro. We rented several rooms for a couple of nights, then set out to explore the town. We bought souvenirs and ate supper in a cool restaurant that featured a live trio band. The restaurant had a big sculptured dragon coming out of the wall. We had calzones, which I had never eaten, and they were so big it was hard to finish them. We visited the Catholic church there, which was built in 1540. It was almost all stucco coated adobe brick.. The roof timbers had to be imported. Wood was so scarce that the ceiling was made of sliced saguaro cactus covered with mud and then painted. It had not rained there since the time of the conquistadors.

The tiny creek that ran through the town was tapped for irrigation water by the local farmers for the vegetable gardens that they cultivated along its banks. The town had grass and trees, and we found they were flood irrigated every week or so by water piped over the peaks of the Andes mountain range about fifty miles away, where there were rain forests on the other side. It amazed me that the combination of the mountains and prevailing winds could create such differences in climate in just a few miles.

The next day, we toured the Inca ruins just outside of town and were told that this was the farthest south that the Inca Empire extended. Then we drove further into the desert and saw the brine lakes where flamingos migrated to every year. We learned that flamingos are actually white but get their pink color from the brine shrimp they live on while wintering on the salt flats. It was an unbelievably barren place with gigantic crystals and sharp clumps of salt poking out of the ground everywhere. It was very windy, and a minor sandstorm obscured some of the distant volcanos and mountains. We were at a pretty high altitude and could tell by our labored breathing.

We then drove on to a national park called Craters of the Moon. There was a big dune of black volcanic sand that was about five hundred feet high towering over many unique rock formations that lit up beautifully as the sun began to set. Later, back at the hostel, we took showers, being mindful of the signs limiting our water use. In the morning, we headed back home to Antofagasta, our vacation feeling all too short.

Mark gave devotions in the morning, and it fit in with what we were feeling. The work felt like it was going in fits and starts, but we needed to be patient and realize that all is part of the Lord's plan. Becca volunteered to have devotions for the next morning, and I wondered what she would have for us.

My host family father was taking English classes through his work, which encouraged the employees to become bilingual. One night I sat down with him and got out my dictionary and looked up words for phone, electric, water, rent, groceries etc., as I was interested to see how their expenses compared to ours back home. Many of their expenses were similar to ours. Food cost less, but water cost way more because of the climate. The biggest difference was rent or mortgage expenses. They only paid $320 in US dollars monthly for a three bedroom, two bath apartment. They lived quite well on his $18,000 in US dollars per year salary.

When we were back at work, we removed the forms on the columns that had been poured just before our mini vacation and reused them on the columns yet to be concreted. We had to go back and fill in a few voids in the concrete and clean out some of the electric boxes where it had seeped in. Mark continued to be the guy manning the cement mixer. His leg was bothering him quite a bit, so he had to take it a bit easier. We had to hold up work a couple of times until a truck could come with more sand and gravel and Portland cement. Ironworkers arrived and set up their work table and began repetitive bends of reinforcing rod to begin making the cages that would go inside the horizontal forms between our poured columns. We knew we would do well just to finish pouring the vertical columns.

On one of the last nights of our stay, the grandkids and I traveled down to the big sand beach where a number of vendors had set up booths selling souvenirs. One young man was doing drawings of people as they sat and posed. He was not very busy. I thought that would be fun, so I asked if he could draw both kids on one sheet and if we had enough time. He said he could and it would only take a few minutes. We chatted as he sketched, and I told him I paint with acrylics. He was an excellent artist and drew rapidly with charcoal. The likeness of the kids was astounding. I paid him extra in pesos because I was extremely pleased. He gave me a set of charcoals and said I should try doing some drawings. We picked up a few more trinkets at the booths and then headed back to our host families.

The last day of work inevitably came, and we reluctantly packed up our suitcases of tools for the bus trip out in the morning. We were due for a special treat that night. Nidia and her husband, who lived right across the street from the church, were hosting a steak roast and party for us as a thank you and a going away present. Nidia was a dietician and had a doctorate degree. Her husband was a doctor of psychiatry. She was Catholic, and he was Lutheran, but Sheryl had become good friends with them when she was stationed in Antofagasta as a missionary a few years before. On our first trip to Antofagasta a few years before, Kimm and I stayed at her house. Her three kids attended Sunday school at the church. Her oldest son, Nicolas, was graduating and thinking about going into law back then. He had since become quite active as a leader in the church. The party was awesome. They cooked up more food than we could eat. The host mom where Mark stayed belonged to an organization that put on shows of native Mapuchi dances. Her group entertained us for over an hour. It was a great time.

In the morning, we loaded up the bus with our luggage and bid everyone goodbye. There were no dry eyes, and many came to the airport to see us off. Becca really cried. She had had four years of Spanish classes and really became attached to the friends she had made. Soon we were winging our way home, happy with the memories and all the new friends we had made. Several weeks later, we got pictures over the internet showing the newly poured floor that they had finished after the good start we had helped them with. Since our departure, I believe the church erected a mostly steel second story on the new floor and that the church continues to grow. I get e-mails almost weekly about events and activities at their church.

Arauco, Chile

January 2012

T he old luggage came out of the closet. Midge and I looked it over to
see if it could make yet another trip overseas. We decided that some
of it would still work, but at least one new piece of luggage would
have to be purchased. We were both excited about the upcoming short
term mission trip to Arauco, Chile. It would be my seventh mission trip
to Chile but Midge's first.

Midge and I were in our first year of marriage. The honeymoon had
been the past spring where we drove out west to Montana and visited
many national parks, and now we were planning on a January trip to
Chile to help a congregation rebuild their earthquake damaged church.
She relied on me a lot to answer her worries about what we would be
doing and what we should take.

Even though the trip was several months in the future, we began
making lists of what to take and things we should buy. Funds were not
an issue for us, as Midge had set aside most of the money we would
need. We got on the internet and found an aerial view of the compact
little town of Arauco, Chile, population thirty-two thousand. We found
out that in Arauco fishing and lumber are the major industries and
that there is a big plywood factory there. Our local lumber store even
imported plywood from that factory in Arauco.

We had traveled to Clarkfield, Minnesota, about one hundred
and fifty miles west of us and met with the team members who were

responsible for putting the trip together. Harvey, Kimm, Todd, and Sheryl, had traveled to Chile a couple months earlier to meet with the church members from the congregation in Arauco.

New Life Alliance Church in Clarkfield had an amazing track record of putting together short-term mission trips. This small twenty-one member church had helped fund and organize perhaps a dozen trips over the years, involving nearly seventy-five different people, many going multiple times. We all felt the need to go to Chile due to the major earthquake that they had had a year previously. It was the third strongest earthquake ever recorded on earth, and it occurred only a couple of months after the much-published quake in Haiti, which killed over two hundred thousand people. The quake in Chile was many times stronger than the Haiti quake but resulted in far fewer casualties due to much stricter building codes and better Tsunami warning systems in that country. About eight hundred people died in the Chile quake, many from the resulting Tsunami that reached one hundred feet high in some areas.

Bob Hepekoski, the Alliance missionary in Chile, had matched our team with the Arauco congregation. He said that they were quite discouraged because they had to tear down their badly damaged wooden church and were meeting in a double garage. He felt out of all the needs among the dozen or so Alliance Churches in southern Chile that had sustained damage, the Arauco church could best be served by the skills of our team. There was still a great underlying fear among the congregation of more severe quakes because of the continuing aftershocks.

The four-person preparation team, with the encouragement of the local Clarkfield Alliance pastor, traveled to Chile. They met with the pastor and the church elders in Arauco to see if we could be of help and what skills and financial aid we could offer. If they were open to our assistance, the team would try to determine the best time to go and how big the work team should be. They needed to iron out where we would stay and how we would be fed and get all other logistics in place. They would also need to get a handle on what work we could do to help so we would know what tools to take with us.

The Arauco congregation was highly encouraged by our offers of help, so all arrangements were made. Team members from the U.S.

and host families in Chile eagerly awaited our arrival, scheduled just after New Year's Day in the middle of the Chilean Summer. We began to connect by email with our assigned host families so we would know what we could take along as gifts for them for supplying our housing and food needs. With the help of funds the team forwarded to the congregation, they poured the slab the new church building would sit on and began to gather materials we would need to begin construction.

A big concern voiced by my wife, Midge, was the language barrier. I had to keep reminding her that I had been to Chile several times, and with the help of a Spanish-English dictionary, a notebook, a pencil, and an ability to pantomime, we would do very well. A few of the Chileans spoke passable English, and we could also take our laptop because it had the ability to translate for us. Kimm's wife, Sheryl, was the Spanish translator for the team, as she had served nearly twenty years as a missionary in Chile. She had retired from mission work to marry Kimm, whom she had met on one of our previous mission trips to Chile. Sheryl was also a former high school student of mine when I taught school in Echo, MN. I promised that it would be great fun. We had hoped we could also use the "speak-translate" feature of our cell phones but found out our system would not work in Chile to get the internet. We took our phones and chargers along simply for their picture taking abilities.

Our trip was scheduled to leave the day after New Year's Day. We discovered that because of the holiday season we could take only one 40-pound suitcase without paying extra. Because of all the tools I planned to take along, we would most definitely be paying the extra fee. Upon the return trip, however, we would be far enough past the holidays that we could again have two pieces of luggage. We purchased a hanging scale to weigh everyone's luggage to stay within the weight limits

Rich Wagner, one of our team members who joined the team late, belonged to Midge's and my church, Eagan Hills Alliance. Rich ran into a snag at the last minute and was not able to find his passport. He was distraught, as he wouldn't be able to get in on the original group purchase of tickets. I encouraged him not to give up and told him that if the Lord wanted to have him come with us, he would be able to expedite his passport in time and that he would still be able to buy a ticket on our same flight to Santiago. He said he would try, and all worked out so that he could still be part of our team. It turned out, I think, that he even got his ticket cheaper than the rest of us. It was evidence of the Lord's hand, as Rich was a valued member of the team, and we would not have been able to accomplish all we did without him.

The day of departure finally arrived, and everyone met at my house. As in the past, I had extra drivers lined up to take us to the airport and drive the team's vehicles back to my home for storage during the trip. After a lunch together, we drove to the airport, where we were dropped off in plenty of time. We worked our way through long lines to get our luggage checked and then went through security to check through our carry-on luggage. Finally, we got to our proper gate for our flight to Dallas. In Dallas, we simply went to the gate for the daily flight to Santiago and had another wait. The Santiago flight was an overnight flight starting about nine at night and going till early morning.

The Santiago flight was on a large jet. The coach seats did not tilt back very far. Midge and Mark each had problems with back and leg spasms and didn't get much sleep at all. By the time we landed in Santiago, we were all running mostly on adrenaline, and we still had another short flight to go to get to Concepción. We had to go through customs and security again to get aboard our short in-country flight on Lan Chile. From Concepción, we rode a bus to the town of Arauco. The ride was along the coast which afforded beautiful views of the ocean and

the forests. The road was very hilly. We got to see beautiful forests of eucalyptus and pine trees growing straight and tall. While on our bus ride, we got to chat with Pastor David from the Arauco Alliance Church and the contractor, Theo, from the church, who would be working with us.

The bus delivered us to the site of the church, where we met our host families and got to see the progress of construction to date. Theo and his helpers had completed the poured slab and some masonry work at the front of the church. Part of that was partitioned off for tool storage. We separated out our tools and left them at the church and then loaded our remaining luggage in our host families' cars for the ride to their homes. Kay, Patti, Midge, and I got to stay with Daniel and Roxanna and their two girls, Connie and Isadora. Other families took one or two team members each. Pat and Kay shared a small upstairs bedroom as did Midge and I. We all shared a common bathroom, which was a challenge at times. Early on, we set up our laptop to help with communication with our host family. They were wonderful at meeting our needs for food, beverages, laundry, and transportation, as they took us wherever we needed to go.

Daniel was very proud of his Chevy Aveo, and even though it was small, he would pack us all in to get his wife to work at the prison, where she served as a guard, and to get the four of us to the church for our work

there. Then he would go to work at a kayak factory, where he and a partner built molded plastic sea kayaks. A few days later, he gave our team a tour of his factory and explained how the kayaks were made; it was quite interesting. In the winter, he worked at another factory, which converted old wine and whiskey barrels into furniture, such as seats, cabinets, wine racks, and clocks as well as various other pieces. It was January–but in the middle of the Chilean Summer, as the seasons are opposite in the southern hemisphere. It gets cold enough in Arauco that every house has a gas heater or more commonly a wood stove because of the abundant sources of firewood.

On day one, we had a devotional to start the day off right. I think I was the first to volunteer to lead. I talked about opportunities God puts in our paths to witness to others and to help those in need. We prayed that we would recognize these opportunities when He put them in our path and that we would have the courage to reach out to others.

We then met with the pastor and Theo, with Sheryl translating, to plan out the day's work. The slab sure didn't look like much of a church yet. We got to view the plans, and we discovered that the majority of the work we would be doing would be the steel framework for the main sanctuary as well as rebar forming and building the concrete beams at the front of the church. That part was mostly masonry, so we would work with concrete, too.

Theo was primarily a contractor who worked with wood and masonry, and he hoped our team would teach him how to do welding so he could finish the work we would start on the main sanctuary. First, we swept the concrete slab and snapped chalk lines on the concrete for

the pattern of the three large steel trusses we had to build. For cutting the steel U-channel, angle iron, and flats, we had three 220-volt disc grinders. We had to cut hundreds of short pieces that had to be welded into place in between the big U-channels to create the webbing, which would give the trusses their strength. When completed, each truss would stand twenty-one feet high and span the thirty-five foot width of the slab. This would make the sidewalls about twelve feet tall and the slope of the roof quite steep. We had to weld steel triangles up the outside of the roof slope pieces for the purlins (horizontal roof braces). The purlins would be welded by Theo on to the triangles after the trusses were erected.

Todd and Kimm welded nonstop for four or five days to get all the webbing assembled. Mark cut steel with the grinder, going through many grinding wheels. I also helped cut steel with the grinder, catching my shirt on fire three times from the sparks. The big Lincoln welder worked the best, but we also had two smaller welders. Before we finished the beams, we had burned out one grinder, one welder, and melted the 30-amp breaker into its slot in the electric box. We ran all those welders, grinders, and battery tool chargers as well as our laptops off of one 220-volt 30-amp breaker. Harvey, the electrician, just shook his head. We should have had at least twice as much power to run all that equipment.

Each day began with breakfast with our host family and then a trip to the church. The ladies of the church served us coffee, cookies, and fruit about every two hours and then made us a lunch of sandwiches, often soup, drinks, and bread with cheese or manhar (sweet caramelized bread spread). After lunch, it was back to work with the steel until suppertime when our host family would come to pick us up. Often congregation members would come to help if they could get time off work. Many worked at the plywood factory, the chief employer in town.

Sheryl, Pat, and Kay spent some time ministering at the prison. Because of the earthquake, the authorities had transferred out all but a few non-dangerous women offenders until it could be repaired. The women in our team also pre-coated the steel parts with primer to prevent rust.

Because steelwork was not the ladies forte, they looked for other projects and found the churches' old pulpit, which had sat outside for nearly two years getting weathered. They glued on a piece of trim that had broken off when the pulpit fell six feet from the stage during the quake. Amazingly, the glass communion set inside the pulpit survived unbroken. With a few hours of sanding, staining, and varnishing, the pulpit looked better than new. On Sunday after church services in the double garage, we went to the town square to pass out a couple hundred Spanish New Testaments that Todd had brought. They were supplied by the Gideon's, and Todd was a member. It was difficult to walk up to perfect strangers who didn't speak English and talk to them about Jesus. Midge went with me, and we gave out about a dozen Bibles and had a nice chat with a Chilean lady we met. She had a

small booth and was selling books. She could speak passable English, so we told her why we were in Arauco and told her about the church. It was fun using our phones like photo albums to show people pictures from back home.

Theo had never had so many workers working under him on a project, and so he was often absent, chasing down more cement or steel or welding rods to keep us in supplies so we could keep working. Theo was so glad we were there as he had little experience with welding steel and was eager to learn so he could put the purlins in place after the trusses were built. Often, when Theo was out gathering materials, we ran out of work and resorted to organizing tools or sweeping the floors. Midge and Mark both became a bit frustrated, and Midge even commented that if we spent all that money to come down here to sweep floors this was going to be her last trip. I said that the Lord put us here for a reason and to be patient.

Midge and Todd were sent to the hardware store one afternoon to get a new big push-broom to make cleaning up the concrete slab easier. Midge was worried that she would not be able to explain to the storekeeper what she needed to buy because she didn't have her dictionary along to translate. She remembered what I had said about pantomiming, so when she got there, she got the clerk's attention and pretended to sweep the floor. They understood right away and gave her the bristle part of the bottom of a broom. Again, she acted out, "Where is the handle?" and then they brought that out, too. Stores sell them separately in Chile. When she checked the bristles, they were too soft, so she fingered her hair and pointed to the bristles shaking her head no. They understood right away and brought out one with stiffer bristles for concrete sweeping. She already had dollars converted to pesos, so she knew how much to pay. She was so proud to be able to communicate and no longer worried about being able to converse with people. Her pantomime greatly entertained the storekeepers.

At last the day came when we were ready to erect the three trusses we had assembled. We had worried that Theo would not be able to find a truck with a lift or winch on it to do the lifting. The trusses weighed about five hundred to six hundred pounds at least, and it would be quite dangerous to stand them up while pulling them with ropes. Because of all the earthquake reconstruction that was going on in town, we could not buy, rent, or borrow a cement mixer, air compressor, or any other tools that would have been helpful to have. Luckily, Theo found a truck to do the heavy lifting, and we tied on several ropes to help hold the trusses up and keep them plumb while braces were welded in place to hold them steady. Many congregation members gathered when the trusses went up, and tears of joy filled a number of eyes, as they could see that the church finally was coming together. From the street they could plainly see the tops of the trusses projecting above the fence around the property.

When she saw the reaction of the parishioners, Midge came to me and said, "I get it now. We are doing this for them, not for us." When she saw how high the trusses projected into the air an idea came to her.

After talking to Sheryl and the pastor, Midge asked, "Wouldn't it be great if we could make a cross to hang from the first truss so that people walking by on the street could see that the church was coming back to life?" The idea sparked interest from the pastor and the team.

The pastor showed us where the old lumber from the church was piled and said it would be very fitting if it could be made from some of the old lumber from the original church. Midge found some rough four-by-fours from an old doorway that had a depression in them from the old hinges and said it would be perfect. I finally got to use my woodworking tools, and we cut a half-lap dado joint into the two pieces. We screwed them together and mounted a loop of rope at the top to hang it. Mark used his grinder to rough up the surface. He and Midge stained and varnished it. After Todd and Kimm welded the braces on our host father, Daniel, climbed the truss, and we threw him a rope, which he looped over the top so we could hoist the cross up. It was a highpoint of the trip when Daniel raised up and hung the cross. We called him monkey boy for the way he scampered up the truss.

Back at our host family home in the evenings, we sent emails home to friends and started a post on Facebook. We used the computer to translate conversations between our hosts and us. Midge showed our

host's two daughters, Connie and Isadora, how to make magnetic bracelets. We had also packed a loom for making potholders with lots of extra loops, but the girls had those all used up within a couple of days. One day Midge offered to cook a traditional American meal. It was a fine meal of beef roast, mashed potatoes, gravy, and corn.

With the trusses erected, work began on welding together the forty foot-long purlins that would support the steel on the roof. Theo directed our team to hoist them up above the trusses and set them in place. Later Theo would weld them to the triangles of steel that stuck up like the plates on the tail of a Stegosaurus dinosaur. These would be further X-braced between each truss for rigidity so that any future quake could not do damage to the roof. I was able to get busy erecting the floor joists that sat on top of a long steel beam we had erected across the front of the church. These would support a future second floor containing Sunday school rooms. The masonry rooms in the front of the church would serve as an office, kitchen, bathroom, and a small nursery or Sunday school room. Theo planned to convert one of the lower rooms into a garage for the pastor's car sometime in the future when the upstairs was finished. We understood that sometime soon we would be invited back to help frame-in the pastor's house, which we would attach to the rear of the church.

Rich from our team worked most of the time with Victor, a seventy-five-year-old wiry congregation member, who directed the rebar and formwork in the front of the church. He prayed that he would live long enough to see the church completed. Eventually the day came to pour the concrete into the wooden forms that contained all the steel re-rods wired together. We formed a bucket brigade to pass the concrete up to the horizontal forms eight feet above the floor. We used a concrete vibrator to help clear out the voids and air bubbles out of the concrete. We used black volcanic sand to make the concrete . Because we were unable to find a mixer to rent, we mixed all of the concrete on the ground with shovels and hoes. It was backbreaking. Later, Victor tried to teach us how to throw sand-mixed concrete against the walls to make a stucco-like finish. We all tried it. Harvey even accidentally threw some out the window, landing it on the pastor's wife. We all agreed it was a skill that would take a lot of practice to learn.

After we finished all the steelwork we needed a bit of a break, so we hired a bus to take us to Lodi, a small town about forty-five minutes up the coast. We wanted to see the old abandoned underground shaft coal mine, but it was closed to visitors.

We went to a gift shop, where we bought jewelry made from cross stones. This special stone has an image of a cross running through it, so jewelry made from it has a religious significance. Then we went to a park that Chileans consider a national treasure of Chile.

The park covered perhaps one hundred acres and ran out on a point into the Pacific. It was created back in the mid-1800s by a wealthy Englishman who owned the coal mines in the nearby town. He traveled extensively around the world and brought back all sorts of exotic trees, bushes, and flowers for the park. He created the park as a playground for his children. He made provision to bury his children in the park upon their deaths. There was a grotto in the center of the park and pathways leading everywhere. There were many employees who kept the park manicured and clean. Officially, the park was closed because the gazebo, greenhouse, and entry buildings were badly damaged in the earthquake and were still being repaired, but we were allowed in as a special favor. The trees and shrubs were all labeled as to species and place of origin. It was a treat and a very special afternoon.

Theo took us all down to the ocean to show us a house that he had built for some wealthy folks a few years ago. He was pretty proud that it had withstood the Tsunami, as the house next door had been destroyed. I was amazed by the corrosion caused by the salt air to all the ironwork on the house exterior. He said that the people only use the house for maybe a month during the year and that they had quite a bit of trouble with thieves breaking in and stealing appliances. It was a beautiful house, which he finished inside and out in wood like a cabin.

Back at the jobsite, we had a pretty windy day, so the small bathroom building that we had erected began to lean. After the door embarrassingly popped open, we had to put a hook on the door to keep it shut. It had a sink and a flush toilet and was a lot nicer than an outhouse. We tacked up a can for donations of pesos for toilet paper and supplies. We got to eat on picnic tables under a canopy right next to our worksite. The church ladies cooked in a neighboring garage. Another neighbor let us use her Wi-Fi address for our computer.

The next to the last day of our trip was on a Sunday, and we had services in the open-air roofless skeleton of the church, with temporary pews set up. The congregation members gave each of us tokens of appreciation, and many tearful thank-yous were shared. I felt moved to get up to speak, and I joked that I was sorry we could not stay longer and solve the bad ventilation problem caused by no roof on the church. Everyone laughed. Then, more seriously, I told the story of a previous trip to Temuco, where we built a tiny little tin church that looked more like a yard shed.

"In spite of the church's small size and rude appearance," I said, "the Mapuchi pastor had shed tears of joy when it was completed." I told the congregation that I said to Pastor Sid, "I could paint a sign so that people would know it was a church." I said that he thought that was a wonderful idea. I asked Pastor Sid, "What should it say?" Then I told them that he said, "Paint on it, 'Templo de Evangelismo'(Temple of Evangelism).

They listened as I shared how bad I felt that to us it was a tin yard shed, but to him it was a cathedral to do God's work. I broke down telling the story and could hardly go on with the lump in my throat and tears in my eyes. Sheryl was translating, and she teared up too because she felt what I felt. She had been there twelve years before as a missionary and translator for the team that built that church. I managed to say that even without the building, even though it is important, they are a church because the church is the people and the building is only a tool to be used to bring more people to Jesus.

Later, Theo invited the congregation and our team to his house, which was just outside of town. We had a fine meal and lots of fun. Nicko, Theo's son, had a laptop, so they were able to find a site that had karaoke

words and music, and Midge got to sing several songs. We all helped to shell garden peas, and I got to taste raw barnacles; they are really bad. The fishy flavor was way too strong. I think they diced them up and put them in the empanadas the next day. It was a fun party.

The final day of work was only a partial day, and we had to sort and pack up all our tools. We left lots of them for Theo to use for finishing the church. We still had to weigh our luggage for the trip home, but we knew we could each have two 40-pound pieces of luggage. We said our final goodbyes and rode the same bus back to the airport in Concepción. The pastor and several others rode with us so they could say the final goodbye. Kimm pointed out the spot in Concepción, as we rode along, where there were a number of twelve story high-rise apartments. He explained that when they had arrived a few months earlier for setting up our trip, one of the high-rise buildings was on its side. It had tipped over and fell onto the ground from the earthquake but was intact. Wow–that had to be some shaking! As we passed by, we could see that it had been demolished and they were beginning reconstruction.

We did a little shopping in downtown Concepción for souvenirs, and then it was off to the airport for our long flight home. We all wished we could have done more but that maybe the best thing we did was to give them a lot of encouragement. We committed to returning to help them build a house for the pastor.

Arauco, Chile

November 2013

Our mission team of eight and our airport drivers sat down to enjoy a send-off meal at a popular buffet-style restaurant. We were only a few hours away from boarding the flight, which would take us to Dallas and then on to Santiago, Chile. There, we would board a Lan Chile flight for the final leg of our trip to Concepción, Chile, where we would climb on a bus to take us down the coast on a two-hour ride to Arauco.

The team consisted of Todd Cole; Harvey Roepke; Pastor Doug Clevenger; and his wife, Carol; Kimm Jacobson; and his wife, Sheryl; Pastor Doug's good friend Dan Brobst; and myself. We were eager and ready to go to work on the next phase of this project, which would be framing in the new parsonage attached to the back of the church. As I shared in the previous story, our team had traveled to this church less than a year before. We had come to help them get started rebuilding their church, which had been severely damaged two years prior by the 8.8 Richter scale earthquake. The city asked them to tear down their church because it was too badly damaged to be repaired. They had hoped to salvage the lumber and rebuild but found that termites had made that impossible. The congregation was quite discouraged and tired of meeting in a double garage.

The team, consisting of many of the same people from the first trip, was returning after less than a year to offer more help. It was easy to make plans because of the willingness of their congregation members to house and feed us and the fact that we had gone through the same procedures only ten months previously.

What was not so easy, for me at least, was to come up with the funds that we would need on such short notice. We did not find out that they wanted us to come back so soon until late summer. I was in the process of retiring from my construction work and learning to live on just Social Security and my rental income, so funds were tight. I had learned from previous trips that if one's heart is right, the funds will be found, so I put the finances in God's hands. I felt strongly led to go again and really wanted my wife, Midge, to go too, but she wanted to stay behind because of the upcoming holiday season.

I placed a call to Pastor Doug in Clarkfield and told him I really wanted to be on the team but that I would need a bit of time to put funds together. I knew they needed money right away to get a good ticket price. Doug recognized my strong desire and said he could carry the costs for a few weeks on his credit card. I had faith the Lord would provide for me but that I would need to get busy and be His instrument to raise the money.

First, I composed a letter that I sent out to everyone on my email address list and explained why we were proposing going on the trip. I asked for prayer support and financial support if they felt moved to help. I thought this would bring in lots of support. It didn't. Several people helped with what they could, but we were in the middle of a recession, and the response was woefully short of the need. Several gave funds designated to buy building materials, as the Clarkfield Alliance Church was also trying to raise funds to help the congregation with that as well. Amid my gloom at the results came the good news that Doug was able to get us round trip tickets including the in-country flight for fourteen hundred U.S. dollars This was a savings of five hundred dollars less than the cost of the previous trip to Arauco.

I still felt the Lord would come through, so I made a trip down to the local shopping center where there was a store inside called Minnesota Arts and More. A couple of years prior, I had placed a dozen or so pieces of rustic diamond willow furniture that I made in their store to be sold on consignment. Few things had sold in the past year, but I was hoping to increase sales, so I popped in and found Jim, the owner.

"Jim," I said, "I have a short-term mission trip to Chile coming up soon, so let's lower the prices on my stuff by twenty-five percent and see if we can sell some things to help me raise funds." "Okay," Jim said, "but you do know that your dining-room set sold, don't you?" "Really?" I questioned. "What is my share, and how soon will you issue the check?" "Fifteen hundred dollars will be sent to you by check in two weeks," he replied. The Lord provides in mysterious ways.

We still had a month and a half left before the trip, and the funds were there. The Lord had provided for my fare, but He had even more to show me. I had written a book called *Keep on Paddling,* which is about my adventures in the boundary waters over many years. It was a compilation of over fifty short stories about things that had happened to me in the North Woods. There was a weekend reunion and rendezvous coming up for the Northern Tier Canoe Base staff and alumni at Ely, Minnesota, on Labor Day weekend. As a former employee of the camp, I asked if I could peddle some of my books at the reunion. I thought it would be a good chance to sell some copies of my book to my old canoeing buddies.

Midge and I; our granddaughters; Midge's son, Dave; and his wife, Cassi, all piled into his Yukon and made the trek north to the base. We had about fifty dollars in change and a couple boxes of my books. We had a good time at the base selling lots of books on Saturday and Sunday at the rendezvous.

We finished out the Labor Day weekend in Motley, Minnesota, at a pig roast hosted by my good friend Dan. At the party, more books were sold. When we got home, we had over one thousand dollars in our change box. Praise the Lord! I sent the first installment to Doug for my tickets. Later, with the extra money I had made on the book sales, I was able to contribute some to the building fund and to buy some of the tools and materials after we got to Arauco. I shall digress, but I felt it was important to share that the Lord can work to exceed expectations and that He will provide.

We left the buffet restaurant and made the fifteen-minute run to the airport, where we rapidly unloaded and said our farewells. We headed to the airline desk and checked in quite quickly. Soon we were lounging at our gate, waiting for our flight to Dallas. We always became a bit nervous that the planes would be late because in at least three instances in the past an entire day was lost because of it. All planes were on time, and in two hours, we arrived in Dallas. Then we boarded our overnight flight to Santiago and were soon dozing away.

We had about thirteen hours of actual flying time on this trip as well as nearly ten hours of waiting in airports before we were finally on our bus for the final leg of the trip to Arauco, Chile. We met with Pastor David and Theo, the construction supervisor, as we dragged our luggage out to the bus, as they had arranged to take us on the last leg of the journey. We walked out into seventy-five degrees and sunshine, quite the opposite from the cold we left behind in Minnesota, as seasons are reversed in the southern hemisphere. They were so happy to see us. Theo was the head contractor for the church construction project and a long-time member of the Arauco Alliance Church.

After grinding up and down the coastal hills along the ocean for two hours heading south, the bus pulled up in front of the church, and we unloaded all of our luggage. We marveled at how far along they had come on the sanctuary. Ten months before, we went home, leaving them with only the steel skeleton of the building erected. Now they had the steel roof and walls up. Theo had closed off the gable ends of the building. He and his helpers had built the stage and windows graced the walls. They had paneled the inside walls with plywood paneling. Theo had installed a functional kitchen and bathroom. There were only two small Sunday school rooms and no office yet but that would come with stage three of construction. We unpacked our tools and separated out the luggage that would go home with us to our host families. We spread out and labeled our tools, organized them for the start of work in the morning, and locked them in the storage room.

We placed cell phone calls to our host families to take us to their homes. I stayed with Daniel and Roxanna and their two teenage girls, Connie and Izzy, again. Dan Brobst, Pastor Doug's friend, was my roommate on this trip. Dan was from Ohio and had never been on a short-term mission trip before. Dan and I had spent quite a bit of time talking about mission trips, and in particular, we discussed the previous trip to Arauco, so he was somewhat familiar with what it would be like to move in with a Chilean family. Dan and I were quite tired from traveling. We turned in fairly early even though we wanted to stay up and talk to our hosts. My wife Midge had shared her cold germs with me as she kissed me goodbye, so, of course, I started to come down with a bad cold. That made it even more imperative to get some rest.

In the morning, we had juice and instant coffee; no one brews coffee in Chile. Breakfast often consisted of pan (bread), mermelada (jelly), or cheese. Sometimes we had manjar (caramelized milk) as a toast topping. Often, fruit was on the menu as well. In Daniel and Roxanna's family, both daughters needed rides to school, both parents worked, and Dan and I needed rides to the church. The poor little Chevy Aveo really got a workout. Four adults and two teenage girls make a full load, but they managed to get us all in, and off we went each morning. Daniel dropped off the girls at school, then jumped out at the kayak factory, where he worked. Then Roxanna took us to the church and dropped us off, then drove on to the prison, where she worked as a guard.

We had to wait a bit for all team members to arrive, as the first morning can be a bit mixed up. We planned for eight o'clock devotions and a nine o'clock work start. I volunteered to have the devotions the first morning.

When I was packing for the trip over a week earlier, I was pondering what to take as gifts for the family. My good friend Craig Kinderman had dropped by our house with something he had found that he thought I could make to sell perhaps. It was a set of three interlocking crosses representing the three crosses on Golgotha.

That night, as I was poking around in the garage and getting tools ready to take on the trip, I found a chunk of an old packing crate that I had saved because I thought it might be an exotic wood. The wood was quite weathered grey, but I knew it was not a native species. I ran it through the table saw and shaved off one side and discovered the wood was bright red orange and it was a species called bloodwood. I thought about Craig's gift to me of the crosses, and it hit me; this is perfect. I proceeded to cut the wood up into one-inch-square strips in pieces long enough to make the cross set and then dadoed them to fit together. I had enough wood to make nine sets of crosses. I decided to take them unassembled and also take along small containers of glue and varnish. I would give them as gifts to the girls with instructions that they must assemble them, finish them, and then give all but two away.

I would also use this as my devotion. I showed one of the piles of unassembled pieces to our team and declared, "This is a puzzle, a mystery. See if you can solve it." Within a few minutes it became apparent how the pieces fit together. I explained, "This was an old, grey piece of wood that looked like it was fit only for firewood, but inside, it was a thing of beauty. It is like our lives, We are but filthy rags because of sin, but if we let Christ work on us, we can become a thing of beauty." The wood was bloodwood–how fitting, as Christ died and shed His blood for us. I spoke of salvation and its mystery and how we must work it out for ourselves, but in reality, it is simple–the cross. The team listened as I explained how the cross is a symbol or a reminder of what Christ did for us.

"The cross," I said, "is empty because He rose again. There were two thieves crucified too; one accepted Jesus and believed and was saved."

When I give the kits to the girls to assemble, I will insist they give them away to others as a witness and said, "This is what we should do with the message of the gospel as well." The team really liked my devotions and thought them very meaningful.

Theo arrived after devotions and took our team to the new concrete slab behind the church to show us what the project would be for our team. Behind the church, but butting up to it, was a concrete slab about twenty-four feet on a side. Theo explained in Spanish, with Sheryl interpreting, that this would become the pastor's house. He showed us the plans for a three-bedroom, two-bathroom modest house. We had many questions, such as "Why aren't there more windows?" and "How do we brace a wood structure for earthquakes?" Windows were limited to six and none on two sides because when they build right up to the property line, windows are not allowed on those sides. He said we would brace all the corners by dadoing in one-by-fours diagonally to make the walls more rigid. A big pile of full cut two-by-threes had already arrived, and we were all eager to get to work.

We put on our nail aprons and "tooled up," getting out all our battery powered saws, drills, and chargers. We had taken nearly one hundred pounds of three-inch Torx screws with us and planned to assemble as much as we could with screws for extra strength. I was in my element, as I am a carpenter first and foremost. The last trip to

Arauco, we mostly worked with steel, and I felt like it was not my area of expertise. Our first task was to attach a base plate to the concrete slab by threading the quarter-inch-thick anchor rods mounted near the edges of the slab through holes that we would drill through the two-by-threes. When the quarter-inch-thick rods were threaded through the holes, the rods would be crimped over and driven back down into the wood for a sturdy bond to the concrete. Tar paper strips separated the wood from the concrete. The lumber was not treated for rotting but was treated with insecticide to prevent termites from taking hold. Soon we had the solid wood base mounted that the walls could be fastened to.

 We began marking and laying out the stud patterns for the walls, but the cooks intervened.

In Chile, people ate at least six times a day. The trick for me was not to eat too much at any one time. The cooks had put out a coffee break spread of coffee, tea, pop, and juice for drinks and bananas, nectarines, grapes, bread, jelly, and cookies for snacks. We had eaten breakfast only a couple of hours before, and lunch followed two hours later, but who complained? This was a daily ritual for us mid-morning and mid-afternoon.

After eating, we were encouraged to put on sunscreen, as we were pale as ghosts from our Minnesota winter's lack of sunshine. In Chile, the ultraviolet rays were especially intense, and often the ozone hole they talked about opened up over Chile, making the sky the most intense blue I had ever seen.

As work on the walls continued I was blowing my nose a lot and running a low grade fever. My cold was getting worse, and I was coughing a lot and going through a lot of handkerchiefs. I was dosing up with decongestants but was still hanging in there.

Each person's skills were becoming apparent. Carol had become cook's helper and our communication expert. She ran the laptop I had brought down and downloaded pictures and put them on the website and Facebook to share with others back home. Sheryl was our chief interpreter. Dan and Harvey headed up the electrical wiring team and began wiring in a new big breaker panel in the church and one for the house. The rest of us carpentered under Theo's direction. I did a lot of the cutting for Todd, Doug, and Kimm, and they assembled. Theo scrambled to get more wood delivered to keep us in materials. We took several thousand dollars with us for them to buy materials, which was added to the money we had forwarded to them a month or so earlier.

By the end of the first day, we had most of the outside walls erected for the first floor. Reluctantly, we put away our tools and wended our

way home to our various host families. Four families were housing two at each location. Back at Daniel and Roxanna's home, Dan and I presented the family with our gifts. Dan gave the family a big quart crock of real maple syrup from Ohio. I gave the girls the cross kits. We set up the laptop on Google translate so I could communicate with them what I would like for them to do. They got busy right away gluing the cross kits together. Then Izzy wanted to play Scrabble. It was a challenge doing the words in two languages. We had our usual late-night snack and turned in. Dan found some meds that he had taken with him to Chile that helped me sleep without coughing all night, much to my relief.

In the morning, another team member gave devotions, and Theo and Maria, our cook who lived across the street, were there early enough to join

us. Sheryl interpreted for them and Pastor David. After our devotion time, we headed back out to the house project. Harvey and Dan worked on planning out the church circuitry.

Before noon, we had all the outside walls erected and braced. We began assembling the inside walls of the bathroom, kitchen, and living room. We had to build the kitchen wall with sockets to accept quite a sizable beam, which would carry the weight of the second floor. We began setting in place the floor joists. In Chile, I found that they used two-by-sixes for joists, even for those spanning up to twelve feet. It would not meet code in the USA, but it works here because no snow load has to be added, and they are full dimension cut.

Lunch was a big bowl of typical Chilean soup. Each bowl contained a half ear of corn, carrots, potatoes, celery, onions, and sometimes other vegetables, then chicken or beef, and of course, the ever-present and pervasive cilantro. Excellent soup! Also, bread, meat, cheese, cookies, and beverages finished out the meal. Well-fortified, we went back to work and began putting down plywood for the upstairs floor.

I pulled Theo aside and told him I would like to get started on the stairway so it would be easier to get up to the second floor. He thought that was a good idea, but he wanted to build the treads of good heavy plank and have them sanded and varnished. I knew that would take a long time and involve gluing up planks, as the steps turned the corner and had triangle shaped treads. I told him it would look nice but would be time consuming. I suggested a cheaper and faster alternative would be to make them entirely out of plywood and carpet them. It would be quieter too, especially with the pastor's two little ones running up and down. Surprisingly, he agreed and then explained how the stairway had to run. They started out straight but then had to turn one hundred and eighty degrees.

I enlisted Todd's help, and we began right away. The first five or six steps would be easy, as it would be a straight run. We took some two-by-six planks for stair jacks and cut triangles to screw to them to make the rise and run of each step. We built three stair jacks and mounted them in place and cut treads and risers for each step. Using screws made everything easy. If we made a mistake, it was easy to

disassemble and correct. The next six steps were like triangular pieces of pie, and each had to be individually laid out. This was much more difficult, so we could not finish that day. The rest of the guys got all the plywood screwed down on the second floor.

The next work day, Todd stayed home sick and vomiting. I was still suffering with my cold but could still work. Sheryl took a bus trip to Temuco to visit friends, whom she hadn't seen in a few years. She served as a missionary there when I went on my first mission trip to Chile. Pastor Doug became my helper, and we finished the stairway. With the stairway built, it was much easier to carry materials up to the second floor, allowing the project to move along more quickly. Some rain had moved in, so we moved inside to help with the wiring and worked outside when we could to finish all the blocking and bracing.

When we could not be outside, we worked inside the church sanctuary helping Harvey and Dan with wiring. Our two electricians installed literally hundreds of feet of plastic conduit and began pulling

wire to all the outlets, switches, and lights. Wiring was a big job, indeed, and we still had to wire the house. We had to take paneling off the walls and partially disassemble the platform to put all the conduit in place.

The weekend was upon us, so we worked Saturday. Sunday, we had church services with the congregation, and then our host families entertained. Daniel didn't speak much English, but he gave us an arm wave and said, "Come on!"

Daniel, Izzy, Dan and I jumped into his Aveo. The two of us did not know where he was taking us. He drove up the coast to the west for a half hour or so and took us to a long stretch of beach. We walked the shoreline, picking up lots of sea shells. Then we came upon a seal on the sand that let us walk right up to him and take his picture. Pretty exciting! He barked if we got too close. Daniel then showed us several cabins that his boss at the kayak factory owned. He rented these out to vacationers. Back in Daniel's car, we chatted about all the different kinds of cars I had seen in Chile, and I mentioned a couple that I had never heard of before. Daniel snorted, "Made in Cheena (China). Junk!" He liked his Chevy!

A little geography lesson is in order. Chile is a country nearly three thousand miles long and about one hundred and fifty miles wide at its widest point. The Andes mountain range makes up the entire eastern border of Chile and the Pacific Ocean the west. Northern Chile is home to the Atacama Desert that is by far the driest place on earth. It has not rained there in at least five hundred years of recorded history.

Southern Chile fades into fjords much like Norway and reaches nearly to Antarctica. Half of Chile's sixteen million people live in a fifty-mile-wide band including the capital, Santiago and the cities of Valparaíso, Viña del Mar, Reñaca, and others.

Chile's climate is controlled as much by latitude as by the Humboldt current in the Pacific Ocean. Chile has dozens of volcanoes, many of them active and is the eastern perimeter of what is called the ring of fire. Chile has many earthquakes as well as the ensuing tidal waves. Two of the largest earthquakes ever measured in the world happened in Chile. Our project was the result of an 8.8 Richter scale quake that occurred only a couple months after the big one that hit Haiti in 2010. Chile had only about eight hundred casualties because they build houses and buildings to handle Tremblers (quakes). Even though the quake in Haiti was much weaker, the casualties were tremendous because building codes there do not take into account the possibility of quakes.

The quake that hit Arauco lasted about three minutes. The epicenter was about one hundred miles south and west out in the ocean. It was so violent that you could not stay on your feet. Most concrete buildings outside walls withstood the shaking because of the extensive use of reinforcing rod, but the back-and-forth action was so strong that many buildings had the roofs sloughed off and had interior walls collapsed.

Arauco has about thirty-two thousand people, and about one hundred were injured by the actual quake. Three people drowned in the ensuing tidal wave. Except for a geographic quirk, Arauco would have ceased to exist. The coastline of Chile faces west until you get down to Arauco. There the coast makes a big hook of perhaps thirty miles with several big islands at the point of the hook. Arauco lies in the inside curve of the hook. The quake happened about one hundred miles south, and the ensuing tidal wave rapidly moved up the coastline. The islands and the hook dampened the power of the Tsunami, so the waves only reached the edge of town. On the coast below the hook, it was another story. Daniel wanted to show us.

Daniel drove us to a hillside around the point of the hook that overlooked a brownish, grassy river bottom. We could see the Pacific twelve miles in the distance to the west. He pointed at our feet and said, "Tsunami stop here."

I asked, "It came twelve miles inland?" "Si." Then he continued, "Come on!"

We got back in his car, and he drove another twenty minutes or so and took us down to the coast at the mouth of the river where there was a small fishing village of about two thousand people. It was right on the ocean, unlike Arauco, which is at least a mile or so inland. Every building was brand new. At the intersection of the new road and bridge into town were hundreds of crosses.

I asked, "Casualties?" He explained, "Nada. All escaped into the hills. These are from the cemetery that was washed away just like all the houses. The government is helping them rebuild. I asked, "How high was the Tsunami?" Daniel replied, "Thirty-meters!" Dan and I looked at each other in amazement. "That's about one hundred feet high," I gasped. I told Dan if I lived here, it would be way up in the hills, not down on the beach.

We wended our way back through the farm and forest country and back to Daniels's house. On the way, I pointed out a large factory of some kind just off the road. Daniel explained that it was the Arauco

Plywood Plant, a mill where many people from town work. I said I would like to take a tour, and Daniel explained that it was in the plans for us to do that.

On Monday morning, we were at work again, putting up the walls on the upstairs floor. There would be four small bedrooms, a bathroom, and a large hall area for a computer set up. This house was kind of a "design as you build," so Theo and I mulled over the wall, door, and closet layouts for the best use of the space. The big problem was with windows; two of the bedrooms had no access to walls into which we could install them. We opted to install three skylights. One of the bedrooms would have a window opening into the hallway. Not the best situation, but the best we could come up with under the circumstances. Theo was open to ideas, so we suggested putting half walls around the winding stairwell to keep it visually open and less claustrophobic as well as make it easier to carry up furniture.

We also suggested size and positioning of closets. The amount of lumber put into the structure was phenomenal. We were getting low on long screws and started using nails on some of the blocking. We fastened three sets of horizontal cross-blocks between studs on all walls for extra fastening points to strengthen the exterior rigidity when we would put the sheeting on.

The next few days, we hand-built about a dozen trusses out of one-by-fours, screwing all the webbing together. Because we built right to the property line, the roof had to have a slot built into it to carry a metal drain gutter because nothing could project past the wall.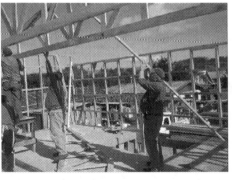
That really complicated the truss building, but finally the team finished putting them all up. Now we could install the purlins. Again,

we only used one-by-fours, but they were nailed quite close together. Without having to worry about snow loads, all roof construction could be quite lightweight. Then we fastened the steel roof on, and we didn't have to worry about getting wet anymore.

The next step, and the last thing we were able to do, was to mount the four-by-eight-foot, thin cement board sheeting around the first floor. We had enough to get only that far. Theo and his helper would have to finish the second-floor sheathing. By that time, another weekend was upon us, and Monday would begin our journey home.

During the week, we had taken half a day to visit the plywood factory. What an interesting place! The number of trees they worked with was a sight to see. We found out that they made several kinds of pine and eucalyptus plywood, some of which was even sold in local lumber yards back home in Minnesota. The plywood was a high-grade pine called AraucoPly. They sold the plywood to about a dozen foreign countries. They also produced knot-free, finger-jointed pine casing and brick molding for window and door trim.

The plant made pulp for two kinds of high-quality paper. The waste wood, delivered in truckloads, was shredded and burned for power, as there was lots of unusable debris from the logging industry. Over thirty-three hundred people worked at this factory, and three hundred of them, mostly women, worked in a nursery, developing seedlings for replanting forests. All their waste water was carefully treated so when it was released back to nature it had no impurities. The plant was modern as well as both

safety and environmentally conscious. Our only disappointment with our tour was that our particular guide was not authorized to take us inside the plant to see how the plywood was actually made. We hoped that we would get to see the inside of the plant on our next trip back.

Sunday came, with the promise of the day being special. Todd had taken about one hundred new testaments in Spanish with him from home on the trip. Our intent was to go to the city square late in the morning and distribute them to anyone who would like one. It sure didn't take long to give them away, and most people were quite appreciative to get one.

After that, we all trekked down to the ocean. Pastor David was going to baptize Theo's daughter and two other church members in the Ocean.

There was singing, preaching, guitar playing, and quite a large crowd of congregation members. I think the whole congregation turned out even though it involved about a half-mile hike through sand dunes. Everyone was taking lots of pictures. The timing of the immersing was a bit critical with the four-foot roller waves coming in. None of the participants wanted to get knocked off their feet. It was a lot of fun.

Then all the participants and congregation gathered again at the church for a big banquet meal of steak and potatoes. We exchanged gifts and tokens of appreciation. Our work team gave out forty Arauco-Clarkfield partnership tee shirts. Besides the small thank-you tokens of thanks the congregation members gave us, everyone took dozens of pictures in every possible combination of poses. We took many pictures by the church sign that Carol had painted. My host family's daughters,

Connie and Izzy, gave out their completed crosses to the other four host families. We began the difficult task of saying *adios* to the church members.

Monday, we met back at the church to pack up the tools that we were taking back with us. We gave the rest to Theo to use on the church. We had to carefully pack and weigh our luggage again so we wouldn't go over our fifty-pound limit.

Pastor David and several others rode to Concepción with us to do a little shopping and say the final goodbyes. We went right to the airport and dropped off our luggage. Several members of the team had no desire to shop for souvenirs, so they stayed behind to guard the bags. The bus took the rest of us downtown to a mall, where we shopped for a couple of hours.

I found a gentleman who made interesting copper jewelry out of scraps of copper wire. I bought necklaces and earrings for the granddaughters. I also found some cute handbags and beach towels for them. For Midge, I found a Lapis Lazuli cross on a necklace. Lapis is a semiprecious gemstone found only in Chile and Afghanistan. I also bought a set of earrings that were made of a special stone found only near Concepción, which has an imprint of a cross in it when it is cut. Then we took a city bus to another good shopping spot, which was a little closer to the airport. We were about all worn out from shopping, so Pastor David suggested we walk to the airport instead of taking another bus. "Only ten minutes," he stated.

Forty-five minutes later, and at about the end of our strength, the airport finally came into view. We didn't mind at all the hour and a half we still had to wait for our flight, as it gave us a chance to rest up.

What a wonderful adventure we had doing the Lord's work with His people in just a short period of time! We almost hated to leave, but we were anxious to get home even though we had heard through our emails that they had gotten fifteen inches of snow back in Minnesota while we were gone. How blessed we felt for having been there and being able to help people who were so appreciative! We had made so many new friends and had renewed many friendships from our previous trip.

We hoped the pastor's home could be finished quickly and that the congregation could raise more funds to complete the house and church building as the church membership grew. Our team left without completing the finishing touches in the house interior and building the stairway to the second floor in the church building, where offices and Sunday school rooms were going to be located. We agreed that we would all love to return and help again with the final bit of work.

Ocean City, New Jersey

⎯⎯⎯ ⧟ ⎯⎯⎯

2014

To continue to encourage the mission spirit that the Clarkfield Alliance Church was so known for, a summer short-term mission trip was proposed by the board members. They wanted to assemble a team to go east to New Jersey to help in the rebuilding of homes damaged during the superstorm, Hurricane Sandy, which struck the northeastern states in 2012. New Jersey was the hardest hit state.

The hurricane damaged so many homes and many were still unrepaired. It would take a decade or more to complete the monumental task. Kimm and Sheryl Jacobson from Clarkfield Alliance Church contacted several organizations involved in the rebuilding, and a plan began to come together. A number of organizations were participating in the home rebuilding process. We joined forces with the United Methodist Churches in the area, which have some of the best-organized plans to help people.

Pastor Doug announced information about the proposed trip at the Clarkfield church at Sunday services. Additionally, he sent other invitations by email. People who had an interest in going were contacted and Doug asked them to pray about whether they felt God was asking them to go on such a trip. The team leaders arranged for us to stay at Lighthouse Alliance Church in Tuckerton, New Jersey. Our commitment was: to work for one week on a project house or houses to be named later. We would have to travel up to an hour each day to the work site.

Early in our planning meetings the team talked about possibly flying out to New Jersey, landing in Atlantic City or Philadelphia, but the team decided costs would be too expensive. Driving seemed to be the best alternative.

Initially thirteen people committed to go, but ultimately only eleven were able. The team consisted of three married couples, Kimm and Sheryl Jacobson, Todd and Nancy Cole, and Midge and me. In addition, there was Ross Rieke, Harvey Roepke, Dan Brobst, Doug Kass, and Pastor Doug Clevenger. One of the team members, Dan Brobst, drove from Ohio where Pastor Doug pastored a church a few years ago. Doug's friend Dan arranged housing where he lived in Ohio for the second night of car travel for those who wanted it.

Midge and I left for the east coast two days early, planning a mini vacation on the way out. On our way we were treated to a free supper by one of the motel managers. We had explained to him why we were going to New Jersey and what we would be doing. He wanted to thank us for the good thing we were doing to help those in need. We got to see Gettysburg, Hershey, Valley Forge, and Philadelphia, all in Pennsylvania on our way to Tuckerton.

Todd and Nancy planned to vacation in New York after the project was over and visit their daughter. Midge and I planned to visit my sister and see a few more sites on our way back home after the project as well.

By Sunday afternoon, all had arrived in Tuckerton in assorted vehicles. A team work planner gave us a tour of the Church facility and he told to help ourselves to the kitchen. He showed us the men's and women's quarters where we would be sleeping on cots. The church had many bathrooms and three showers for us to use.

An insurance company rented out part of the church which assisted in paying the mortgage. I believe the church also received some financial aid for putting up the volunteer workers. We had to buy our own food and the work organizers asked us to contribute one hundred dollars each to help buy materials for the project.

There was a lot of cooperation between churches. The Lutherans cooked one breakfast and a supper during the week for us.The Lighthouse Church fed us pizza the first night. The Methodists had the project organized and had a coordinator named Paul, whom we would meet on Monday morning.

We found our project was to be in Ocean City, on an island that had become awash with the storm surge–up to four feet deep in places. The last storm that was nearly as bad was in 1944. We had two houses we could work on about two blocks apart, and both needed sheetrock and flooring.

The coordinator had supplied a portable biffy which was placed nearby. The previous teams electrical work was only partially inspected in one house and the earlier teams plumbing had to be finished in the other house before we could install sheetrock.

Paul gave us the okay to use our team as best we saw fit, so we thought we would start on the house that had part of the electrical work finished so we could sheetrock at least some of the ceilings and walls. We were able to order whatever we needed from a local lumberyard and have it delivered, or we could pick it up ourselves.

The first day, we worked on hanging sheetrock ceilings in two rooms. I headed up a team of the gals and worked to teach them how to tape the seams and cover the screw heads with drywall cement.

After breakfast each day, we had a short devotional given by Pastor Doug. He was able to use examples from our work effectively. We kept saying mud covers all or mud covers a multitude of sins referring to the drywall work and the finishing compound, and he changed mud to blood and how Jesus' blood covers all our sins. Each day he had something from the Bible that tied into our work for the day.

We had an interesting work dynamic. We had a pastor, two electricians, two contractors, a diesel mechanic, a farmer, an insurance salesman, and three housewives. We ranged in age from forty-six to seventy-one, but most were in their sixties. We were a bit crowded, all working on the small row house that was only fourteen feet wide and maybe forty feet deep. The work became focused on trying to get all the drywall done on both floors in the first house. By midweek, the second house had the plumbing done, but we were really rolling along with the drywall and taping. We decided that the most efficient use of our time was to concentrate on one house.

The work evolved into Doug Kass, the other contractor heading up the sheetrock cutting and installation, and sometimes we split off into two teams in two different rooms. The three gals, under my tutoring, followed the sheetrock installers and taped the seams and covered the nail heads with drywall compound. We ordered plenty of drywall joint

compound; I believe we went through about twelve 5-gallon pails and about forty plus sheets of drywall.

Building codes in New Jersey were similar to Minnesota's, so we didn't have to deal with anything unfamiliar. My team of gals became quite proficient at applying dry wall tape and mud under my tutelage. Midge had the most experience doing construction, as she had been helping me for several years. She also helped teach Nancy and Sheryl how to tape seams. As a team, we were able to get four rooms paint ready, with only minor sanding needed and a first coat on the back bathroom during our week of work. The men were able to get sheetrock hung throughout the entire house, except for on the walls in the upstairs bath by the

end of the week. We all felt if we had only one or two more days, we could have gotten the whole house ready to paint. The people we worked with and the pastors at Lighthouse Church were all friendly and helpful and delighted at our progress.

An elderly black man named Kenny owned the house. He was ill and had not heard the hurricane warnings and was trapped upstairs for several days without food or water during the storm. He was a semi-invalid and was in a care home until his house was finished being repaired. His sister, Loretta, came by every day to check on progress. It was emotional for her to see the work toward completing the house that her brother had been out of for two years. She had been born in the house, and it was over one hundred years old. She gave us gifts of corn and tomatoes from her garden. It was her way of saying thanks.

Ross had rigged up a tarp lean-to, with benches and a table. It made a nice shady spot on the back of the house for us to eat our bag lunches.

Midweek, Sheryl mentioned to me that one of my former students from Echo High School–back in 1975–was back in the lower 48, visiting from her home in Alaska. Sara Alexander was her name, and she was going to drop by and help us for part of a day and get reacquainted with Sheryl and visit with us. What a fun reunion! Sara and Sheryl had been classmates in the high school in Echo, Minnesota, where I had been their teacher so many years ago.

We took off part of a day and went down to the ocean to see the boardwalk and all the stores lining the beach. It was hard to imagine all the damage that was done during the storm from two years ago, as most of the mess was pretty well cleaned up. Many homes, especially of the less fortunate folks, still remain badly damaged inside. Our project supervisor, Paul, dropped by nearly every day, and by the end of the week, he was happy with our progress and said we had moved the project two weeks closer to being done. More groups would follow us to finish the remaining sheetrock, painting, flooring, and kitchen cabinets. He said it may take up to ten years to help all the people in need to get back to how they were before the hurricane.

We were all given tee shirts for our efforts during the week. Midge and I both felt positive about this trip and could only wish we could have stayed longer to get more done.

Sadly, since I have written the story of the trip to New Jersey, we heard from Loretta. Her brother Kenny passed away in his finished home. His heart gave out, but at least he had a few months to live in his completed house before he went on to his forever home in heaven. May he rest in peace.

Guadalajara, Mexico

—◦◦◦—

2015

Sheryl Jacobson from Clarkfield, Minnesota, had gone on many mission trips to Chile. She had spent a good part of her life there working for the Christian and Missionary Alliance Church. She sent out an email that reached me in late March. She was in contact with Cheryl and Bob Fugate and with Sharon and Tim Greenfield, who had been missionaries in Chile for many years. As a denomination, the Alliance Church in Chile had become well established, and they were even sending out their own missionaries to other countries.

To make the best use of the manpower resources, the Alliance had moved almost all the missionary couples to other countries to try to be most effective in spreading the gospel. Thus, Sheryl had found out from the Fugates and the Greenfields that the Alliance Church had reassigned them to Guadalajara, Mexico. They were trying to establish a fourth Alliance Church to be named "Breath of Life" in the southern part of that city of four million people. Sheryl was told by the Fugates that they had a core group of three families who had rented two buildings in an unused resort complex. They hoped to hold their first church service about the middle of April. Sheryl thought that maybe a team could be assembled quickly to help the missionaries with the many tasks of getting ready for the opening of the church. The problem was that it was planting season and a busy time for most of the former team members who worked in agriculture.

Kimm Jacobson and Harvey Roepke, the faithful electrician, said they would go. Dan Brobst, a friend of Pastor Doug Clevenger from Clarkfield, also joined the team. Dan was a veteran of mission trips to Arauco and to New Jersey. Due to the short notice, I did not think I would be able to go. My wife Midge and I had many complicated commitments in the month of April, including closing on the sale of a home to our son. Initially, I said I would be unable to go when the dates were announced. Midge knew I really wanted to go and made some calls to make arrangements to sign papers early. About a week before departure, I saw my way clear to join the team.

I have never seen a trip so attacked by the devil and so in need of prayer! Kimm and Dan bought their tickets right away. Harvey was still awaiting the arrival of his expedited passport, so I waited to buy my tickets along with his so we could travel together. His passport came four days before departure, and Pastor Doug purchased tickets for Harvey and me. We found our flight would go to Chicago, then to Houston, and then to Guadalajara. Dan and Kimm, who had gotten tickets a week earlier for a little less money, were scheduled to fly to Denver, then to Houston, and then join us finally on the last leg of the flight to Mexico. We all worried a bit because of all the connections we had to make. If any flights were delayed it might be tough to get to the proper gates quickly enough to make our next flights.

Everyone met at my house in South Saint Paul on the day of departure. We weighed our luggage and loaded it all in Dan's Pickup. We carpooled to the airport and made arrangements with my wife to be pick us up on our return. We waited together at the airport until it was time to be separated. We paired off in two teams of two, going in different directions to get to the same place.

Harvey and I did okay, just making our second flight to Houston by only a few minutes. Upon our arrival there, we looked at the big flight board and saw that Dan and Kimm's flight was delayed from Denver. Soon it was apparent they would not make the final connection and would be stuck coming in a day behind us. Then it was announced the Guadalajara flight was to be delayed, so we thought they might make it after all. Finally, they announced that there was no pilot available for our flight, so it was cancelled.

At this point, the boarding line became the voucher line for food, lodging, and taxis. Soon after the line formed, Kimm and Dan's plane arrived, and they appeared across the concourse. We waved them over and gave them the news. We waited in line for three hours before we got meal, motel, and taxi vouchers as well as new tickets for a flight in the morning to Guadalajara. As a team, we discussed and then voted to stay an extra day because of our delay.

We notified the missionaries in Mexico we would arrive in the morning. We had trouble finding a cab that late at night at the airport. When we finally got one, the driver took us to the wrong motel. He soon came back because, luckily, we had given him the wrong voucher. We straightened the voucher up, and then he took us to the right place. At one in the morning, the bed felt very good, but we knew we had to arise early to take the motel shuttle to the airport.

Refreshed with a continental breakfast in the morning and a short two-hour flight, we finally got to our destination. The problems did not stop, though. While we were traveling, the missionary team found that the woman who had rented the buildings to them for the new church had sold the buildings. In spite of the missionaries having a prepaid contract and putting in over forty thousand U.S. dollars into building repairs and modifications, the owner had sold the property out from under them to some unscrupulous buyers, who ordered them off the property.

Our team arrived, but the property we had intended to work on was lost. Those in charge decided that pursuing legal action would take too long and be unprofitable to the church, and there was a possibility of danger since it was rumored that a drug cartel had bought the complex of buildings. Paying bribes to judges to get quick justice was not an option.

After meeting our host families, Bob made arrangements for our team to help the east side Alliance Church set up a facility to train pastors. The missionaries at that church, Steve and Debbie Zopfi, were trying to develop a seminary and had a couple of rooms at their church that needed fans, lights, bookshelves, and some air conditioning work before they could be used effectively. We all felt that at least our trip down would not be a total waste, so we went right to work. Kimm and I modified the metal bookshelves to fit the spaces allotted, and Harvey and Dan began running conduit for the wiring.

We had a late lunch and worked until dark, getting quite a bit done. Then we went out to eat with the missionaries at a local restaurant. There Dan and Amber Marcello, the newest missionaries in the city joined us.

I was housed with Arturo and Roxanna, one of the core members of the new church. The rest of the team members stayed with the Fugates and the Greenfields. Arturo was a famous Mexican guitarist who puts on about eighteen concerts a year playing for two bands. They were a wonderful, interesting couple, who treated me like I was royalty. Arturo practiced his English on me, and he was quite fluent. We had many long discussions about many topics, and I even found a little time to show him how to paint with acrylics, a hobby he was taking up. I struggled with a relapse of my chest cold and found that the altitude of sixty-two hundred feet was a bit bothersome. My sleep was interrupted often by coughing and trips to the bathroom.

In the morning, we had breakfast with our hosts and then were taken back to the east side church to continue working, a drive of about an hour in heavy traffic. We did find that the city was more Americanized than anything we saw in Chile. They had many of the same hardware stores and restaurants we would see in the US.

We finished running most of the conduit. Dan and I began pulling wire and wiring in outlets and switches. We were also replacing or abandoning some of the old unsafe wiring. Kimm and Harvey moved into the small office, put up three or four lights, and then ran more conduits for a fan and switches.

We had not seen much of our team leader, Bob Fugate, as he was working hard to solve the problem of having no building for the new church. A friend of one of the core family members had discovered a nearly finished brand new building in the right area for the church. Tile and painting were done and all that was left really was part of the wiring. We had two electricians on our team. Fredricko, the owner and contractor, was excited about our interest in renting his building for the church. Bob had made an offer to rent the second floor, which included a full apartment, a large meeting room, a kitchen, and three bathrooms. It was only a few dollars more than the older property they had lost but was so much nicer and needed less work. Bob took us to see it in the morning. The best news of all was that they would get back all the money they had invested in the first property, which amounted to over forty thousand U.S. dollars.

We had the opportunity to sleep in a little later the next morning, but I did not, as my cold continued to be a bother. I snuck downstairs and sent an email home so that Midge and the prayer warriors at church would know that their prayers were effective and not to stop. I emailed that we would have an exciting day, as we were going to see the new property. After a short while, Arturo and Roxanna came down, and we had eggs and toast for breakfast–along with bacon he had purchased special for me.

The new property was only about twenty minutes away, and we all arrived with our heavy suitcases full of tools. The building's owner, Fredricko, arrived and opened all the doors so we could get to work. The day warmed into the low nineties. Fredricko had brought a watermelon for us to share. He was very nice. He said his mother was ill, and we promised to pray for her. He was raised as a Jehovah's Witness but wanted to leave his church and was looking for the truth. He was eager for us to turn his building upstairs into a Christian church.

We had only two days left to change the empty upstairs into a church. Bob wanted me to assemble a raised platform, and cover it with carpet for the front of the sanctuary as well as a large cross and a podium. He also wanted me to draw out the Alliance Church symbol that was used worldwide and cut it out of plywood. He had his pickup, so we zipped two blocks away to a small lumber yard and picked out the lumber we

would need and arranged to have it delivered. At last I would get to make sawdust! Cheryl went to Home Depot to find carpet for the platform.

Harvey and Dan began hooking up wiring and tracing out circuits. The lights were not hung, and we needed some working outlets for the first church service. Kimm worked on setting up a buzzer with an automatic door locking system. Bob had ordered chairs which were promised for delivery in time for Sunday services. Time was running out to get the building ready. Fredricko had his contractors doing final tile work in the kitchen. Cheryl and Sharon hung up signs and banners. Other members of the core congregation worked to install a projector and computer system.

They were trying to keep up with all the sawdust I was creating while making the platform and cross and soon ordered me to cut the

wood out on the balcony to keep the mess down. women helped by cleaning paint and stucco off the windows. It was a flurry of activity. When he finished the wiring, Dan came down off the ladders and helped me carpet the raised platform. It was made in two pieces that were three-foot-by-ten-foot sections, so they could be carried easily. Bob ordered more wood and I began building the large cross. I decided to make it hollow on the backside so it wouldn't be too heavy to move. I used a grinder to give it a hand-hewn look and mounted it on a base so it would be freestanding.

The podium was pretty easy to make, but the Alliance world symbol took some time to draw and cut out with the sabre saw. I worked out on the balcony so I wouldn't create any more dust inside the church. With my work outside, the crew mopped all the floors. A truckload of padded church chairs arrived. The cushions were all wrapped in plastic, which we had to remove. The helpers doing the removal found it to be tedious. As the chairs were readied, they were arranged around the podium for services to be held the next morning. Exhausted, we all went out to eat after dark and finally got home after eleven o'clock.

In the morning, we were up early and headed to church. We were excited and prayed for a good crowd to come to the first service. Bob hoped for at least twenty to come but perhaps as many as forty. We placed bulletins on the one hundred brand new, maroon-colored church chairs. The Mexican ladies set out punch and cupcakes for afterward. Tim and Sharon set up small chairs and a chalkboard for Sunday school for the little ones.

By the time the church service began, I had lost count of all the people, but I knew we had over fifty. More and more people kept coming in. Soon people filled all the chairs, and there was standing room only. After a couple of songs, the pastor excused the twenty or so little ones to go to Sunday school, and those standing found seats. The congregation filled all one hundred chairs.

Pastor Bob preached. The director of South American missions spoke. The director thanked our team. We sang hymns and choruses and praises to the Lord. The hopelessness we had felt at the beginning of the week with the loss of the property was turned completely around. The Lord had provided an even better facility with an enormous

crowd attending. Indeed, we all felt it was a miracle. Even Fredricko, the contractor, was there as well as a woman from California, who was a long-term resident looking for a church. An older couple, who considered themselves tentmakers, also attended. They were known for establishing new churches, and had a real passion for it. By the time I broke away to get to the kitchen I found the crowd had eaten all the cupcakes and drank all the punch. What a marvelous Sunday!

We got to spend a little time with our host families late Sunday afternoon and even got to take a short nap. Our time was winding down, and we had only one more work day, Monday. Then we would wing our way home. We had all agreed to stay the extra day to make up for our cancelled flight.

In the morning, I went back to the new church with Cheryl and put a coat of walnut stain on the cross, podium, platform, and plywood Alliance symbol. team had built. Cheryl helped with brushing on the stain. The cross looked especially nice. Dan, Kimm, and Harvey went back to the East side church and finished wiring up the ceiling fans and also put lights and a fan in the pastor's office.

Late in the afternoon, I joined them, and we decided to try to install door openers in two more locations. After stringing the wire, we found that the new system had wire that was too light, so a relay would have to be installed to make it work. We were so tired by then we opted to skip supper and head right to our homes to pack up for our flight home in the morning.

We slept, as we were exhausted, but we woke refreshed. I got up early and packed up. I had a second bag of tools and had to pay an extra forty U.S. dollars for it, but I needed all the tools we had taken with us on the trip. My carry-on bag also weighed nearly fifty pounds because I had distributed the weight to keep my other bags light enough to avoid additional fees. At the airport, they inspected my carry-on and said it had to go in checked baggage because of the screws and nails, so Harvey took it as his second piece, and I paid another forty U.S. dollars. I should have just thrown the nails and screws away, which might have been a loss of maybe twenty U.S. dollars, but I didn't think of it.

I tried to sleep all the way home, but my cold congestion kept making me cough. The flight home was much smoother and less eventful, but upon landing at Minneapolis, we discovered two of our pieces of luggage were missing. Mine came to my house the next day, but Harvey's had to be delivered to Granite Falls, one hundred and forty miles away.

I must say this was one of the most difficult mission trips I have been on because of the cold I had and the altitude of the city. The devil was working hard to keep us from our project. This was the closest thing to a miracle that I have seen on any mission trip and one could clearly see the Lord at work. The Breath of Life Church we worked on had grown to an average attendance of sixty each Sunday, according to email reports I got from Sharon periodically. As of the time of this writing, they had remodeled their upstairs to enlarge the sanctuary. I do not think the Lord is finished using Midge and me, and we are open to going on additional trips for Him as long as we are able.

Rockport, Texas

2018

In August of 2017, Hurricane Harvey slammed into the south Texas coast just a few minutes' drive north of Corpus Christi. The sustained 135 mph winds did major damage to a number of cities along the coast, destroying and flooding thousands of homes. The winds slowly abated, but the rains continued to fall as the storm moved up the coast toward Houston, where it stalled for days, where up to four feet of rain fell. The flood damage was enormous, and it will take south Texas years to recover.

A number of disaster relief organizations moved in, along with FEMA from the federal government. The Alliance Church, in Clarkfield, Minnesota, wanted to put together a team to continue their mission spirit. Pastor Doug contacted Samaritan's Purse, which is tied to the Franklin Graham organization, and the Baptist church. In the discussion, we learned that they only had room for four additional volunteers during the week we were planning.

We pared down the team to Pastor Doug Clevenger, Harvey Roepke, Ross Rieke, and me. The trip was about twelve hundred miles each way. We planned to drive down in two SUVs, one of which was supplied by Pastor Doug's entrepreneur son at a significantly discounted rate. We allotted three days for the drive and would arrive on Sunday afternoon at the Baptist church in Portland, Texas. This is where we would be housed for a full week of work, which we would finish on the following Friday. We also allotted three days for the return drive.

At our first planning meeting, we tried to estimate how much the drive down would cost, including motels for the four of us. We estimated we should get to the Kansas City area the first night, Dallas the second night, and arrive in Portland the third night. I mentioned that I had friends in both Kansas City and Dallas and volunteered to contact them to see if they could put us up for the nights going down and coming back. That would save us the costs of motels and maybe some meals. We thought we should each contribute two hundred and fifty dollars toward gas costs. The route down was pretty easy–Interstate 35 the whole way.

Over the next few days, I contacted several of my friends and arranged housing for us all as well as meals. They were willing to help us out in any way they could. We were not sure what kind of work we would be doing, so we packed a few basic tools that we thought might be helpful. Each of us packed air mattresses because the friends we were planning to stay with had room but not enough beds. The Friday departure date neared, and the three men from Clarkfield, Minnesota, arrived at my house Thursday night. Midge treated us all to a venison roast and mashed potato supper. We turned in pretty early, planning for departure by eight in the morning. We loaded up our gear in the Ford belonging to Ross and the Audi, which was rented to us by Doug's son. Harvey and I rode in the Audi. It took us quite a while to figure out all the bells and whistles that car had.

We got a bit confused in Kansas City but managed to find Mike and Karri Roods' house in the suburbs south of the metro area. They gave us a nice meal, and we had a great visit. After we blew up our air mattresses, we turned in again, planning for an early departure. In the morning, we had a nice breakfast and loaded up. We had a prayer for a safe drive, and we were off again, heading for Dallas. As I looked over the map of our route, I discovered we would be going right through Wichita, Kansas, where I had a brother and sister-in-law. A quick phone call led to an invite to drop in. Judy and Larry put together a quick lunch for us. We could only stay for an hour, but we had an enjoyable visit.

My Friend Owen Gibbs lived in a Suburb about halfway between Dallas and Fort Worth. We were able to find his place using GPS on our phones. Owen had hidden a key for us to get in because he had to make an emergency trip to Washington, D.C. He had made wild boar

Jambalaya for us and said to make ourselves at home. He planned to get in a visit when we stayed again upon our return trip. Then we would get to meet his new cat named Jack and his dog named Bonehead. We got a good early start again. As I looked over the map, I saw we would be going through Waco, Texas. I knew that Waco is where the Gaines family, of the TV show *Fixer Upper*, has a big store. We decided we couldn't stop for lack of time but maybe on the return trip.

We drove through Corpus Christi, Texas, late in the afternoon and then crossed the high bridge over Corpus Christi Bay. Just on the other side of the bridge was Portland. We soon found the Baptist church, where we would be housed and fed for the week. I called another friend, John Thurston, who lives in Corpus Christi. He drove over to see us right away for a short visit. We jumped in his suburban, and he gave us a quick tour of the area. We saw the aircraft carrier Lexington that is berthed near the bridge. We missed getting a tour because it was late in the afternoon. John explained about all the refineries and how the oil tankers come in under the high bridge. We told him we would like to have a supper with him and his wife later in the week. We asked if he could find a nice seafood restaurant for us.

Back at the church, we met our team leader, Tim, and the staff members of Samaritan's Purse. Our daily agenda was explained. Tim showed the four of us where the men's quarters were located as well as the showers. The church had a large campus with day care and classes going on all the time, so we tried to not interfere with any of their activities with our presence. We parked our vehicles in the back of the parking lot, carried our gear up to the second floor, claimed our bunks, and made up our beds. Lights went out at 10:00 p.m. sharp and came back on promptly at 6:00 a.m. We had to make our beds, get showered, dressed, and make ourselves sack lunches before breakfast at 7:00 a.m. After breakfast, we had prayer time, devotions, and announcements. The four of us were teamed up with a couple from St. George, Utah, to work on a house in the town of Rockport, Texas. Rockport is about a thirty-minute drive north of Portland and was especially hard hit by the storm.

We met our team leader, Tim, out in the parking lot by one of Samaritan's work vans. He had us climb in the van, explaining that we would ride up to the Baptist church in Rockport. There, we would switch over to a diesel crew cab pickup, which would pull a fifth wheel work trailer to the job site. When we got to Rockport, we loaded up the trailer with ice and drinking water.

The storm had caved in the wall of the front of the church. The church began meeting in a tent that was erected for them until their sanctuary wall was repaired. Samaritan's Purse was planning to build a large dormitory building, with showers and a kitchen, to house volunteers. In three to five years, when they had finished all the repairs from Harvey, they would donate the building to the church.

Once we had everything loaded, we headed to the house we would be working on. We had seen lots of flood and wind damage on the way up. As we drove along, we saw further storm devastation. The live oak trees in the pasture lands were shredded and often uprooted and then rolled into piles. Many highway signs and billboards were bent over or stripped of their panels. There were numerous damaged roofs, caved-in walls, and in many cases, houses were missing entirely. One mobile home was gone, except for the floor, which its owners had well anchored to the ground.

People abandoned many remnants of houses. A half-mile strip of highway median was piled with debris (lumber, metal chunks, furniture, carpet, sheetrock, trees, and waterlogged home contents), which was being  picked through to salvage metal and usable material. The remaining items would be hauled away to be buried. One had to wonder where the people rendered homeless by the storm were staying.

We arrived at the home of a Hispanic family. The grandfather, Juan, owned the house and lived there with his granddaughter and her son. They were staying with relatives but visited every day, eagerly checking progress on the repairs being done to the house. The storm surge in that neighborhood reached about three feet, and Juan's house had knee-deep water inside during the storm. That necessitated removing all the sheetrock and insulation and rewiring the whole house as well as buying new doors, cabinets, appliances, and windows. When done, we hoped the house would be much nicer than before the storm and a lot more valuable.

Previous teams had done all the demolition and cleanup of debris and replaced all of the drywall. They had also repaired and repainted the exterior siding and re-shingled the roof. Our part in the project for the week was to try to complete the interior painting and get all the door jambs and doors installed. Then we would install the casing on the doors and the wood base trim. We also needed to replace a number of missing and broken ceramic tiles in the back bedroom.

The house had three bedrooms and two baths as well as a kitchen, living room, and rec room. Like most homes in Texas, it was one story and built on a slab, with no basement. We knew that we would need to spend a good deal of time on our knees and that it would be a pretty big job to get the 1400-square-foot house all trimmed out. We found out we would not be able to do the window trim, as the new windows were still on order, along with the new cabinets.

Tim explained that Samaritan's Purse had trouble, at first, getting people to even ask for help, because they would have to divulge all of their financial information. They then would have to contribute what funds they did have available to help with the repairs. Samaritan's Purse, then would donate additional funds, along with the volunteer labor, according to the needs of the applicants. Applicants worked with Samaritan caseworkers to determine if their caseworkers could approve their projects. If approved, the caseworkers assigned a team leader, who

would oversee the volunteers working on the project, until the work was completed. Each team leader assigned to an applicant was on salary from Samaritan's Purse. Each team leader had available a pickup pulling a twenty-by-eight-foot gooseneck trailer loaded with every tool imaginable to help complete the project. Most of the projects that the teams worked on were in the Rockport area, which was one of the hardest hit by the storm. Samaritan's Purse also had teams working closer to Houston where flooding was severe. Samaritan's Purse expected to be involved in helping for the next three-to-five years.

We were shown by Tim where each of the tools were located in the trailer, and we unloaded those that we would need. We set the power tools up outside to keep the dust level down. We found that the few tools we had packed from home were not necessary, as the trailer contained

everything we needed. The tools were high quality and well cared for.

Lou and his wife, our assigned teammates, got right to work painting. Tim directed the rest of us in framing up closet door jambs and installing casing around the doors. Harvey started

on getting a few outlets working so that we would not need to run the generator. Doug and Ross cleaned the floors and marked where the vertical studs were in the walls so we could fasten the baseboard securely with the air nailers.

We drank a lot of water, especially on the warmer days, and took morning and afternoon water and snack breaks. We all ate lunch together

out on the front driveway around a small table. On Monday of that week, it was warm enough that we were swatting a few mosquitos. Back home, in Minnesota, my wife was dealing with over a foot of fresh snow. I texted friends to try to get her some help removing the snow.

At the end of each day, usually about four-thirty in the afternoon, we packed up all the tools, cleaned up our area, and then headed back to the Rockport church. We parked the truck near the Samaritan office trailer. We then switched back into the passenger van for the ride back to Portland. We gathered for supper around six in the evening and then had time for showers, reading, visiting, or other activities. Most of us hit the bunks before the mandatory lights out at ten at night.

The routine of each day was nearly the same, and we made progress steadily toward completing all the painting and trim work. A big problem was getting materials delivered to keep us making progress because there was such a high demand for building materials from the local lumber yards. There was some resistance to the volunteer help coming into the area by some of the local contractors immediately after the storm. It soon, however, became apparent there was more than enough for everyone to stay busy for many years. A number of people driving by rolled down their windows and yelled, "Thanks" or "You're doing a great job!" Samaritan's Purse was trying hard to build a good reputation for the quality of their work and their love of the Lord.

On the third day of work, we witnessed another way some folks were addressing the damage from the storm. A few doors down from where we were working, a double wide trailer home was brought in and set up. The delivery man maneuvered the two halves into position onto the slab of a house that had been torn down because of the extensive damage. He did this with the use of a small remote controlled treaded tractor. It was rather neat to witness.

One evening, we were entertained with some volunteers from Utah, who had taken along their musical instruments with them on the trip. It was enjoyable. We hated to have to stop, but work needed to go on. The leaders of Samaritan's Purse asked if it would be possible for us to stay another week. It was too short of notice for us, but we said we would consider another trip down later.

The next morning upon our arrival at the office trailer, we were met by a distraught young woman holding her three-year-old daughter. She asked if we were from Samaritan's Purse. We said that we were, and she told us that she could really use some help. She and her three children were living in a small FEMA trailer that was totally inadequate. She owned a damaged house but had no funds to repair it to make it livable again. We directed her to the office where she met with a case worker. By the time we got our pickup hooked up to the work trailer and got everything loaded, she was heading back to her car with a hopeful smile on her face.

That night, our team skipped supper and drove into Corpus Christi and had a fine seafood dinner with good friends of mine, John and Becky Thurston.

Our last workday, Friday, had arrived. Before we headed to the worksite, Melanie, the volunteer coordinator, had us all gather to get a team picture.We were also reminded to write greetings in the books, which she had set out for each of the teams, on our thoughts on about particular projects. These would be given to the homeowners upon completion of their projects. We loaded our bedding and  suitcases into our vehicles and cleaned out our sleeping quarters in preparation for the new teams coming in the following week. We drove our vehicles to the Rockport church because we would depart from there and head north immediately after finishing up our workday. We were able to complete all the painting, and because one of the Samaritan staff members was able to locate additional trim boards, we were also able to get all base and casing installed. We wrapped up work a bit early and made a special effort to clean up the house, sweep out the work trailer, and vacuum all the sawdust off the tools. We wished Lou and his wife well and thanked Tim for letting us help on the project. As we said our goodbyes, all of the team members stated they would like to return to Rockport again in the future to give additional help.

We headed north to Victoria, Texas, to the residence of the Peterson family, where we had been invited to spend the night and share a meal. I had taken along handmade wooden bowls that I had made on my turning lathe as gifts for all the folks who we had stayed with or who had given us meals on the way down, but I had run out, so I promised to mail the Petersons a copy of another book I had written entitled, *Keep on Paddling*, which is a compilation of short stories about the boundary waters in Minnesota. We had a great visit with these longtime friends and again enjoyed the hospitality of a good meal.

In the morning, we headed north again but drove in quite heavy rain for several hours. My friend John texted me that they had gotten four inches in their rain gauge in Corpus Christi. Later that day, we passed through Waco and decided to stop and visit Magnolia, the store set up by famed hosts Chip and Joanna Gaines of *Fixer Upper*. We shopped for an hour or so and then completed our drive to Euless, Texas, where we found my friend Owen at home with his dog, Bonehead, and his new cat, Jack. Again, we had a great visit, excellent food, and a good night's sleep.

Sunday morning dawned; it was a bit chilly but above freezing. We headed into Kansas and were again able to break for lunch with my brother-in-law, Larry, and his wife, Judith. Then on we went to Kansas City, staying the night with Mike and Karri. That night we went out to supper with them and helped celebrate their twenty-ninth wedding anniversary. Monday, we made good time and were back in the Twin Cities by mid-afternoon. The team dropped me off at home and then turned in the rented Audi and headed home to Clarkfield. A week later, Midge and I drove to Clarkfield and participated in a potluck and a welcome home ceremony at the Alliance Church. The new friends we made in Texas and on the way down will long be remembered.

The story I shared is of our experience with this horrible tragedy for the people of Rockport. We were only but a small part of the effort put forth not only by Samaritan's Purse but also by many other churches of many denominations. Not only churches, but other local, state, and national relief organizations actively came together to assist all of the displaced residents of Rockport as well as many other Texas communities. A true example that when needed, people from all walks of life can and will band together and do what needs to be done to recover from such a tragedy!

Big Sandy Camp

Sign project

Big Sandy Camp, the Northwest District's Bible camp run by the Christian and Missionary Alliance Churches in the Minnesota area, was in need of signage. The camp, under the direction of the late Gordy Fisher, had grown over the years from a small camp primarily for summer campers to a year-round retreat facility with many buildings and services. There was a rickety weather-beaten sign on the road, which directed folks into the camp but little else except some crudely made signs labeling some of the buildings. The Maintenance director wanted dozens of signs made with a uniform style of color and lettering, to not only label the buildings and the road into camp but also to give directions to where different activities were held. We sat down together to make a list of all the signs that he needed, and I was asked to submit a bid.

By early winter, the project was approved, and my friend Craig and I set out to design the signs. My sister-in-law Kate searched the internet for an appropriate font and size to use and did the layout on her computer for the letters for each of the signs. We cut all the letters out of stiff cardboard. Next the letters were traced onto an adhesive backed rubber stencil and then we laboriously cut out each letter. The next step was to apply the letters to the wooden sign blanks.

We planned to sandblast or sand carve each sign in one-and-a-half inch-thick salvaged redwood. Most of the directional signs were uniform in size about eight inches high and three feet long. The building signs were much larger, and the road sign was to be at least four by eight feet. The redwood had to be all heartwood with vertical grain and free of knots. Only a couple lumber yards carried the lumber, but they said they had little left and their stock was very expensive, with no more available due to environmental concerns. Most sign companies that made these types of signs had gone to using a dense foam rather than wood and used a wire grid when they sandblasted to mimic wood grain.

Fortunately, I had a big supply of recycled redwood. The previous September I had attended a reunion of camp staff at the Northern Tier Scout base in Ely where I had worked years ago. The maintenance director there asked me if I wanted the lumber and the metal bands from the old wooden water tanks that the camp once used for storing water. He explained they were weathered and gray and were not used anymore because the new well was able to supply the whole camp. Water no longer was pumped from the lake and stored, so the old wooden tanks were not needed. At first, I thought I wouldn't want the wood until I saw it was redwood and that it was heartwood and vertical grained. I loaded it all up and took it home. The two round cylindrical tanks had each been six foot tall and six foot in diameter. The boards from both tanks all laid side by side would cover an area six feet wide and thirty-six feet long. Each board was only about three inches wide, and the edges were slightly beveled to make a tight seal when banded together.

It was about a six-hour sawing project, which would convert the boards into something usable. First, I ran all the boards through my table saw and shaved off all the beveled edges. Next, I raised the blade and shaved about an eighth-inch off the weathered side to get to clean redwood. I ended up with about a bushel of sawdust. Next, I got out all my long pipe clamps and exterior glue and assembled the clean boards into panels that were about six feet by three feet. After the glue dried and I removed the clamps, I had to sand the blank planks and wipe the dust off of them. I then sawed the big panels into sign blanks of the size and number needed. I had nearly fifty signs to make. I designed each one to have the corners and edges rounded and bordered with a narrow-routed slot around each edge. I then stuck all the cut out stenciled letters and the edge strip around the perimeter of each panel. An arrow stencil was stuck on to give directions. I had to stencil both sides of all directional signs but only one side of the signs labeling buildings.

My next step was to load up the sandblaster with fine silica sand and don protective gear. I turned on the air compressor and I began the sandblasting process. Behind the rubber stencils, the wood stayed smooth because the sand was bounced off. Where the wood was unprotected, the sand ate away the wood, exposing the wood grain. The wood was eaten away by the sand almost like a blowtorch would melt away a block of ice. Many hours and hundreds of pounds of sand later, I completed blasting.

Next I brushed two coats of paint on the blasted parts of the sign. We had chosen hunter green for the background, with the borders and letters in light grey. I carefully painted the accent slot a dark maroon. After I applied two coats of paint to all the backgrounds, then I peeled off all the rubber stencils, and then painted the edges and lettering with two coats of light grey. Finally, I carefully inspected each sign and touched up.

Craig Kinderman and I carefully wrapped each sign in blankets and old quilts and loaded up my van to make the three-hour trip up to McGregor, Minnesota, where the camp was located. Upon arrival, we enlisted help from the maintenance man in finding the best locations for the signs. We used post-hole diggers to dig in the six-by-six posts from which the signs would hang. The directional signs hung down from each other on screw-eyes suspended from cross-arms. The building signs were screwed to the front sides of the buildings. Erecting all the posts and installing the signs took all day.

A couple of years later, we built a large entry sign for the camp out on the road. We also made additional signs for new buildings and for new featured activities the camp had added.

Big Sandy Camp Mission Trip

Work on Fisher Chapel - 2009

During a winter lull, with no out of country mission trips planned, an opportunity came along to do some work finishing off the chapel under construction at Big Sandy Camp. The camp was owned and operated by the northwest district of the Christian and Missionary Alliance Church. In spite of it being owned by the CMA, many Christian and even some Jewish churches avail themselves of the camps facilities. The camp is used year-round for summer camps and winter retreats and is available for family use as well.

The facilities are state of the art and there are lodges, cabins, a gym, a beautiful beach and several meeting rooms. The camp can accommodate several groups at a time. The New Life Alliance Church in Clarkfield, organized a "come when you can and stay as long as you are able week" to work on the new chapel.

The Chapel was named for Gordy Fisher who was a well-loved and dedicated camp director of Big Sandy for over twenty years. He had to retire early in his fifties due to a debilitating early onset of Alzheimer's disease. Just recently we heard he had passed away. He had done so much for the camp.

Big Sandy Camp endeavored to go ahead with projects only after money is raised to do them, so using volunteer labor helped a great deal to stretch the dollar. Six or Eight from Clarkfield volunteered to go as well as myself and my good friend Mark McCoy from the Eagan

Hills Alliance Church. Mark and I planned to give it three or four good days, as we had projects going on at home that could not be put off too long.

The work we needed to do at the camp was build a large raised stage at the front of the auditorium with pipelines beneath the floor to run wiring for sound and other controls. Also, on the agenda was for us to build a large sound booth in the back. For those who could do finish carpentry, there were six doorways and about twenty to twenty-five windows to install extension jambs and casing around. In the hall way, we were asked to paint the wall, trim and exposed pipes. Also, some electrical work up high on the ceiling for the lighting was waiting for the right person to tackle it.

The architects had arranged most of the windows in stacked columns of four high, which made working on the top ones a bit scary at over twenty feet in the air. There was ample wood for the trim. It was pre-stained and varnished birch, so we had to drill nail holes to avoid cracking. We assembled multiple sections of scaffolding to reach the top windows and the ceiling. I stayed below with Mark and cut pieces of trim. Mark tied them to a hoisting rope to get them to the top of the scaffold. The braver team members, Todd Cole, Kimm Jacobson, and Harvey Roepke climbed the scaffolding and mounted the trim and did electrical work. The ladies teamed with others to paint and stain the foyer. We made significant progress on the first day.

The camp staff provided good food for our team and for the workers who had come from other churches. We spent a restful night and the next morning got back to work. By the end of the day, we finished the extension jambs and casing, and then we began work on planning the large stage. We stood long prebuilt web trusses set in place at twenty-four inches on center to get the stage about twenty-four inches off the floor. This would give good visibility to the congregations and groups that would be using the camp chapel.

The team still had to build stairs for ease of access to the stage, and we needed to lay in PVC piping for passageways for wiring. A number of electrical boxes had to be installed for power and microphone connections. Then the steps and topside had to be covered with three- quarter-inch plywood for strength. Eventually the camp would carpet the entire platform. Others began work on the raised sound booth in the back, which would house all the controls for sound, lighting, and projectors.

By day four, our team felt we had accomplished a lot, and most of us had to head back. Some stayed longer if they could afford the time. The guys looked forward to getting to use the chapel at the upcoming Men's Retreat, held each February. The chapel would hold about four hundred, and it would be a joy to use it to sing praises to God. It would be a big improvement and provide much more space and light than the old chapel, which was connected to the back of the dining hall.

Mission Weekend
to District Bible Camp

⸻⸻⸻

Painting project early spring,
2014 at Big Sandy Bible Camp

J ohn Baker, the maintenance man at Big Sandy Camp, sent out an e-mail requesting help with painting all the bunkhouse rooms above the dining hall (Lakewood Lodge). Big Sandy, our district Bible camp and retreat center, would house and feed any volunteers. The rooms were to have ceilings and walls painted, and all rooms needed two coats on the walls. I brought up the idea to a number of the members of the New Life Alliance in Clarkfield and several thought it would be a fun thing to do.

We decided to go up to the camp on a Thursday morning and then work through Sunday and come home Sunday afternoon. We were told by John there were five rooms yet to paint, and they hoped we could get perhaps two or three done. Pat and Jerry Nikoliasen and Harvey Roepke volunteered to join the team from Clarkfield. Including Midge and me, we had five people in total. The camp director, Dave, mentioned that this was the first weekend that no groups were in camp in a long time and all the staff had the weekend off. That meant that cooking was up to us. We would be able to use the camp kitchen and whatever supplies we could find, but we wouldn't have much help from the staff. We decided to still go up that weekend because it was the best free weekend for all of us.

Midge and I bought some groceries for a few of the meals. For the first supper, we planned to eat at the restaurant in McGregor, Minnesota, where we would meet the rest of the group. Pat and Jerry also brought groceries to round out the rest of the meals we would need for the weekend. There was still snow on the ground, and it got deeper as we drove further north. It had been a long, unending winter. We had a nice, all you can eat, fish dinner at the restaurant and, afterward, arrived at the camp in good time. We bunked at Loon Lodge. We looked over the project at Lakewood Lodge and decided we could maybe get all five rooms painted. I had raised the idea of a paint sprayer, which would help with painting the white ceilings. Then we could second coat the walls with brushes and rollers. That night we enjoyed a fire in the fireplace and played a few rounds of the game, Jokers and Pegs.

In the morning, we assembled my new sprayer and masked all the bunk beds that were still in the rooms. We mixed up the white latex for the ceiling, and we finished painting the first ceiling in less time than it took to mask the room. We then moved to the second ceiling. Harvey helped mask because of his height advantage (six foot-two), and the others began painting the walls. In each room, we painted three walls tan and one wall an olive green. To do a room involved finishing two coats on a couple of walls and then shifting all the bunk beds to make room to paint the remaining walls. Each room had wainscot on some of the walls as well as the usual switches, outlets, heaters, and bulletin boards to take down or paint around. We fell into a good routine, and by days end, we had two rooms nearly done. That evening, we had a good hot supper, prepared by the gals, and then we played some more Jokers and Pegs around the fireplace.

In the morning, Midge and I woke up to three deer staring at us through our bedroom window. What a beautiful site! We breakfasted and had our coffee and went back to work. We built on our learning experiences from the day before and worked to try to get all the rooms done. We sprayed all the ceilings first so we could clean up the sprayer and be done with the difficult masking. Then all we had to protect was the carpeting and the objects we were painting around. By that night, we had all rooms done and left the cleanup and loading for Sunday morning. John came back from his weekend and was amazed at the progress. Dave, the camp director, returned Sunday morning and was surprised the painting project was done and expressed his gratitude. After our cleanup and loading of equipment, we had some time to spend looking over the camp, and we decided to check out the newest property that the camp had added.

The camp property was primarily a large, flat, sandy plain with a hill backdrop and a long beach front. It was on the east shore of Big Sandy Lake and had some beautiful sunsets, as the beach faces west. One private cabin was located at the far end of the camp, and the camp had to allow the owners access through the camp to get to their cabin.

When that property came up for sale, the camp board of directors felt it would be wise to purchase the cabin and its acreage to eliminate the access issues and provide another cabin for families or small groups to use. We toured the rustic building, with its rustic furniture, and felt it was a good addition but that it needed lots of work on the roof and the floor to make it more structurally sound. Perhaps another mission project for another time would be forthcoming, we thought.

We had great fun on our mini-mission trip and felt that we accomplished a lot for the camp. When we were ready to leave, we all decided that we were a very awesome team, and Midge and Pat kept spouting it to everyone. I said our team should come back the following year and repaint the dozens of directional signs around camp, as they were getting a bit faded. Everyone thought it would be a good idea.

A Trailer Load of Ladders

March and April 2015

O ften, work for the Lord can happen right at home. In February at the Men's Retreat at Big Sandy, our district Bible camp, I cornered John Baker, the maintenance director. My good friend Craig Kinderman and I have a special love for Big Sandy Camp. We had helped on many projects there, such as siding buildings, constructing a big deck on the waterfront, building a barn to house the petting farm animals, building signage for the whole camp and more.

I had mentioned to Craig that I wanted to propose to John, the maintenance director that we build ladders for all the bunkbeds in the camp to make it easier for campers. Specifically, for us old-timers, it was a bit difficult to get into the top bunks. I would get a chance to talk to him at the upcoming Men's Retreat.

Big Sandy hosts many retreats and summer camps and is busy nearly every weekend year-round. It is our district camp, but they also host retreats and getaways for many groups. They can house multiple groups and can put up over three hundred and twenty people at a time. My ladder idea was an ambitious project, as it could involve one hundred and sixty ladders for all the bunkbeds. Craig could not make it to the retreat, so I bunked with my old mission trip buddies from Clarkfield, Minnesota. Sunday, after lunch, when the retreat had ended and the men were all heading home, I finally sat down with John and explained what I would like to do.

He expressed a bit of skepticism about the need for the ladders, but I explained how tough it was for us older guys to get up and down from the beds, especially when we had to go to the bathroom multiple times during the night. He said we were the only group that ever complained about the difficulty in using the beds, which is why they had put into the registration forms the question: "Do you require a bottom bunk?" He was also concerned about where they would be stored. We came to a compromise agreement; I would make one ladder for each room rather than one for every bed. He wanted to see how it would work out and whether it would be good to make more at some future time. I walked through all the buildings and found I would need over fifty ladders for each room to have one.

I contacted my good friend Jim Krech when I got home. He had a sawmill on his property and several thousand board feet of planed and dried green ash lumber. I thought the wood would work well to make the ladders. I asked if he would like a big tax deduction for the year by donating enough ash boards to make between fifty and sixty ladders. He was happy to help out and said to come over and help myself to his pile of wood. I took my trailer over to his house, and his son Jesse helped me load about three hundred and twenty board feet of lumber.

I cleaned up my shop and picked a day to start the project. First, I built a single prototype to iron out any bugs that might show up. I made an angled ladder with five steps. Each step was ten inches high and fifteen inches wide and three and a half inches deep. The whole ladder would be made of three-quarter-inch-thick lumber, with small triangle braces under the top and bottom steps. I planned to dado all the ladder steps into the sides, using glue and screws together for strength. I tried straps of iron, then regular angle irons, and finally settled on large screw in hooks to hang the ladders on the ends of the beds. The ladders would have a slant of fifteen degrees when hooked on the beds and would be able to be hung on the ends of the bunks when not in use.

After I made the prototype and it seemed like it would work, I gave Craig a call, and he came over to help for a whole day. We ran all the boards through the table saw and cut them to width first. Then we made a repeatable pattern for all the steps and sides. The ash boards were all eight foot long and various widths. We avoided or cut out all the bad spots from the boards. Mountains of sawdust and several hours later, we had one hundred and twenty sides divided into rights and lefts and three hundred steps.

We ran all the steps through the saw and grooved them for traction and to help prevent cupping. We cut scraps into triangle braces. We dadoed all the sides to a depth of three-sixteenths of an inch. Then we drilled and countersunk all the screw holes.

Finally, we could start mass assembly of all the parts. Soon there was little space to move around in the garage. In the next few days, we had all the ladders assembled, and I awaited the arrival of the screw eyes that had to be special ordered. When they came, we took nearly a whole day to drill and mount them all. When all the work was finished, the ladders were all loaded in my small four-by-eight-foot trailer and securely tied and covered with a tarp. A few days later, both Craig and I had a free day, so we drove to Big Sandy Camp to deliver them.

When we got up to McGregor, Minnesota, near the camp, we found there was a good coating of snow on the ground. Upon arrival, we began to distribute the ladders to each room. John caught up to us and helped. I had a bad chest cold and had trouble, as I was getting winded, going up and down the stairs. We found we had made enough for one for every room and two for each room above the dining hall, where there were a lot more bunks per room than some of the other buildings.

We hoped that this project would make staying in camp a bit more pleasant for the participants. Later that summer, John mentioned to me that he had a lot of favorable comments about the ladders. We will find out this year if they would like more of them made. Some mission projects can be done right at home. There is always something that can be done to help keep the camp in good shape.

Should You Go?

———⊗⊗⊗———

I t has been said that the money spent for a person to go on a mission trip would do a lot better if it was just gifted for the work to be done. The thousands of dollars spent on airfare to get a team to a location such as Chile or Nepal or New Guinea would buy a lot of building materials. The costs to get a team of ten or fifteen builders to Chile, for example, could be between fifteen thousand and twenty thousand dollars. Those dollars could buy a lot of lumber, concrete, and other building materials. The last statement is true, but we must also consider things that cannot be bought.

Jesus admonished his disciples to "Go ye therefore and teach all nations, baptizing them in the name of the Father, and of the Son and of the Holy Ghost" (King James, Matthew 28:17). Was He talking only to them? If we are his followers, are we not also included to be his witnesses to the whole world? I believe this verse speaks to us all.

You may not be physically or financially able to travel abroad to witness to others. The phrase "all nations" means America too. Our country, more than ever, needs Christ. Does your neighbor know about Jesus? Does your coworker in the next cubicle need the encouragement only God can give? Does your own heart need uplifting? There is unspeakable joy in seeing someone turn away from their evil ways and follow Jesus because something you said or did spoke to them in a powerful way.

We should all be witnesses for Jesus, but not everyone can or should go on an out-of-country mission trip. You should not go if you are not confident in your salvation. You should not go if you will put your family in need or if you would not be able to meet your obligations and responsibilities at home. You should not go if you will become proud of your work abroad and not give God the glory. You should not go if you cannot make yourself an open vessel for Jesus to fill and to work through. That said, if you have a love for mission work in your heart but cannot go, you can surely give to support those going, and by all means, you can pray to protect them from the assaults of the evil one and to have God bless their work.

If you feel you lack any useable skill for a trip, be advised that this is not an excuse. Moses tried this out with God, and God still impelled him to lead the Israelites out of Egypt (Ex 2:11- Ex 3:17). Peter was a simple fisherman who at one point denied knowing Jesus three times, but under the Holy Spirits power, he preached a great sermon at Pentecost and led thousands to Jesus (Acts 2:1-Acts 2:4). The backward, uneducated fishermen who made up most of the disciples began God's church, a church that today–two thousand years later–has billions of followers. God can mold soft clay to be what He can use. If we are not open to His leading, we are brittle shards who cannot serve any purpose for Him. You don't need to have great skills for God to be able to use you, but you must have a willingness to let Him lead you.

Each of us possesses useful skills for any mission trip. You may be a carpenter or a steelworker or an insurance man or a housewife. God can find something you can do for others and for your team on a trip. Maybe you cannot pound a nail, but you might be able to minister to a troubled soul just by talking to them. Perhaps you are not much of a brick layer, but you could mix the mortar. Maybe you feel you are only a housewife, but you could cook for the team, and maybe your testimony would touch someone in a significant way. Maybe you have exceptional organizational skills that could put together all the details necessary to plan out a team trip overseas.

I have had friends say to me, "Why spend so much going overseas when there is so much to do locally or in our own country?" Often those who make those comments are doing little for the Lord anywhere. If you are truly mission minded, your life will reflect helping others wherever you find yourself. You will find opportunities at home, in your church, in your community, in your country, as well as all over the world. If we reach out to the needy, the hungry, the thirsty, and the unsaved anywhere, then God can and does work through us.

Most of my comments thus far have been about our service to others… what do they need and what we can do for them. I want you to consider this statement. What would a mission trip, especially overseas, do for you? I can answer this only from my own personal experiences. I am a service-oriented person. I like to help others. I like to teach. I did service projects to get my Eagle Scout award. I was a high school science teacher for eight years. I have taught Sunday school in the past. I do, however, have a bit of a problem with pride, even though I try to remain humble. I like the praise I get by helping others. I do like to brag a bit. Hearing people say thank you gives me a warm fuzzy feeling.

But what did the trips I have taken really do for me or to me? I went on my first mission trip to Jamaica as part of a team, and because my wife Kathryn really wanted to go. On that trip my faith was stretched by having to do street evangelism. My feelings about all the things I own and am blessed with were shaken to their roots by seeing what poverty is really like. I came back changed a bit. I refused to believe we could go on the second trip to Paraguay because of the higher expenses, but the Lord worked in miraculous ways to provide what was needed. That trip opened my eyes to the needs of people, and we got to see some marvels of God's creation.

The first trip to Chile broke my heart when the Chilean pastor wanted me to paint a sign for the small, simple, tin shed we had built him for a church. What we thought looked like a yard shed was to him a great cathedral. He wanted the sign to read "TEMPLO DE EVANGELISMO" (Temple of Evangelism). God has given us in the USA so much. Do we thank Him enough? Do we share with others? Each trip I have taken has changed and molded me in ways I could never have imagined. I have encouraged a number of my friends to join me on trips so they too can experience what I have felt.

I have learned a real man can cry. I have discovered I have emotions. I have learned if your heart is right with God, He will provide and He can use you in miraculous ways. I have seen my prayers answered in God's way and time. I have had my sins of pride and unbelief pointed out, and I have seen God point me in the right direction. God has used me in ways I would have never considered possible, often in ways above my skill level or my pay grade. And yes, I still get a warm fuzzy feeling on every trip I have taken. Saying goodbye to the new friends I made was always difficult.

In short, a mission trip will change you in good ways. You will become a different person with a whole different perspective of the needs of a sinful world. You will, as I have, make new lifetime "out-of-country friends" and learn the culture of other countries. You will also give congregations and people who are struggling hope for the future, and you can have great fun doing it. You will make fast friends of your team members.

So, should you go? Give? Pray? Yes… all of these. Above all, open your heart to the Lord and let Him fill you. If you feel the tugging to go and are able, don't say no to the Lord. Do you feel you can't afford to go? Pray and watch him provide. Can't speak the language? A laptop computer is able to translate. The Lord will provide a way to communicate, be it with pantomime and a pocket dictionary. Do you feel you have no usable skills? God knows you are able to do things that you never suspected. Open yourself to the Lord and watch Him do great things through you.

STEM (Short Term Evangelical Missions) was a good way to start out doing mission trips because they take care of planning many of the details. Your own church may have a mission team going somewhere–join it! Maybe you know a missionary who you can visit and help in some way. Do some research, and you can find a team to join.

Can you go and leave your responsibilities at home without bad consequences? Before you commit to going on a trip, consider what the purpose of the trip is. Look at who is going and why they are going. Do you feel the Lord tugging at your heart to go, and is your heart right with Him? Are you still busy making excuses? Why not pray, "Okay, Lord, I am in your hands"? What about tackling projects closer to home? Yes! By all means do these as well, but don't limit yourself. It is a mighty big world out there with a mighty big need to know Him. Never forget He is a Big God.

SAMPLE LETTER OF SUPPORT

<Your Name>   Month, Day, Year
123 Main St
City, State 00000

Dear friends,
I am writing this letter to offer an opportunity for each of you to support
a short-term mission effort to <Destination>.

You may be aware that <Destination> suffers from many hardships and
faces many challenges <Examples>. Many <Denomination> churches
in the country were damaged and some were destroyed or had to be
torn down.

Recently, <Your Organization> has taken interest in assisting the people
of <Destination>. Thus far we have raised <$0.00> to assemble a team
to assist. Our goal is to reach <$0.00>. With these donations, our intent
is to: <Describe project plan, # of members, scope of project, dates of
project, etc.>

The opportunity is there for all of you to support us through prayer,
as we are planning to travel to <Destination> on <Date>. I will be
going representing <Your Organization>. Any funds raised beyond
travel needs will be applied to purchasing additional materials for the
<Destination> project.

Please prayerfully consider a monetary gift to encourage the
<Destination> congregation. Any checks should be made out to
<Organization> with <Project Name> in the memo for tax deduction
purposes. Donations should be directed to <John Doe>

In His name,
<Your Name>

Printed in the United States
by Baker & Taylor Publisher Services